# The Secret World

## of a

## Private Eye

# George Brady

# Acknowledgements

My grateful thanks to Lauren Hughes whose encouragement and guidance in creating this work was truly inspirational.

And to illustrator Mark Letman for his excellent front cover design.

# Contents

# Foreword

**B**y its very nature, the private investigation industry is shrouded in secrecy and mystery. Very few of the populace make it their calling and there are no defined apprenticeships leading to a career in the profession. This narrative is intended to afford the reader a grasp of the craft's intricacies and to open an avenue of insight into the world of the Private Eye.

# Chapter One
## Leaving the Job

How and why did I become a Private Investigator?

To answer that question we must go back in time; back to the time I was a Detective Officer in the Hampshire Constabulary. Back to when I lived within striking distance of London and 'moonlighted' on my rest days for a security agency in classy West End hotels. To when I sat in the bar of the Grosvenor House and engaged in innocuous parlance with an Arab gentleman, the conversation of which led to an offer I couldn't refuse. The deal on the table was a twelve months renewable contract heading up the security at a newly built hospital in Saudi Arabia. The package included a free flight to any destination in the world every four months and a salary to make my mouth water.

It was 1988 and a good time for me to go. My police career was in the doldrums, I was in the middle of divorce proceedings and, frankly, I was rather strapped for cash.

I accepted the offer there and then, and following a few weeks of formalities, resignation and visas etc., I was on my way to the Middle East.

The year I spent in Saudi Arabia managing the security of the King Faisal University Hospital in Al Khobar, in the country's Eastern Provence, subsequently proved to be the way forward. In my absence from the UK, my personal affairs had been in the hands of my brother who had acted as my Power of Attorney and, by the time I had returned, divorce proceedings with my wife had been completed and the dust had somewhat settled. She and our teenaged son, Edwin, were already comfortably settled into their newly purchased bungalow and I was now a free agent. The pot of gold at the end of the rainbow was that I was able to renew the good relationship I had had with Edwin and this, thankfully, has been maintained to this very day.

*

# Chapter Two
## Super Salesman

**B**ut, what to do now? Having been brought up on a strict work ethic in the coal-mining North East, I had never been one to rest on my laurels and I soon set about looking for another job.

During the time I worked in the London hotels, prior to going to Saudi, I had met Kay, a smart, attractive, single lady from Cardiff, who was on a weekend visit to the bright lights with a girl friend. Now I was back in the UK and 'homeless', it made sense to base myself in her home town. This, despite the fact I had never before set foot in Wales; but I knew that whatever road I was going to take was going to have to start from scratch.

Having been a police officer for the best part of my working life, I was now in a position to explore whatever other talents I might possess. The luxuries of freedom and financial independence were now mine to be used to discover whether I was suited to another calling.

My financial situation was crucial to my long term planning. Money was earmarked for a deposit on a new house and furnishings and, of course, I would be dipping into my capital to cover general living expenses until the arrival of my first pay cheque, whenever that might be.

Ever mindful of an Aristotle Onassis quote I had once read, "Most businesses that fail in their first year do so because the owners lack the financial backing to see them through the bad times," I knew I had to ensure sufficient capital was kept in reserve to sustain me in that difficult period prior to the onset of a regular income.

I had often contemplated that I might make a decent salesman. I got on with people and considered myself personable and articulate. So, why not?

A promising advert in the local paper caught my eye – "National kitchen fitting company offers good remuneration to successful Salesman. Full training given." Just what I am looking for, I thought; training, a new career and a good salary.

The interview with the local sales manager brought home the true reality of the situation and I was left with the distinct impression that, as long it wore a collar and tie, a monkey would be offered a job. The position on offer would be on a fully self-employed, commission-only basis with no expenses available under any circumstance. Sales brochures dished out free to prospective clients would have to be purchased from the company out of my own pocket, as would advertisements placed in shop windows and store notice boards etc. 'Training' would consist of merely accompanying the experienced reps on their various visits to possible buyers, which were known in the trade as "prospects."

However, despite these disappointing revelations, I decided to give it a go. After all, I would never ever again be in such an advantageous position to indulge my fanciful suppositions and it would prove to me once and for all whether I had the qualities to be a successful salesman.

Subsequently, accompanying various reps to their 'prospects', I soon learned how mean, ruthless and hard of heart a salesman had to be to accomplish success.

The salesman's first step was to telephone the would-be client who had innocently responded to an advertisement and pressurise him or her into hosting a visit. From then on, a relentless, scheming, formula would be set in motion. It was a well known fact that unless the sales presentation lasted at least two hours, there was rarely a chance of a deal. Thus, the unsuspecting 'prospect', anticipating nothing more than a friendly five minute chat and a quick, speculative estimate, would be inveigled into a lengthy ordeal, culminating in his or her signature on the order form. The salesman knew only too well from experience that if the deal was not done at the time of the 'pitch' it would probably never happen. Blatantly brazening it out, comfortably seated in the client's armchair, he would cleverly overcome all objections with subtle rejoinders, offering "one-off reductions only available on the night" or pretending to phone his manager to obtain "a special price", until the worn-out victim finally succumbed and wearily signed on the dotted line. It mattered not one jot to the salesman whether he was dealing with innocent fledglings or an elderly lady living alone. The only thing he cared about was his commission and, after travelling miles at his own expense and spending hours of his precious time delivering his spiel, he had no intention of leaving without what he considered to be his just desserts.

It took three months on the road without selling a single kitchen to at last convince me I was just not cut out to be a salesman. But the final straw did not come until I actually did make a sale when, unfortunately, the struggling, newly-married couple in their first house did not have the requisite £50. Like a knight in shining armour, I came to their rescue. So anxious was I to earn my first commission and clinch the deal, I offered to pay the deposit for them. The order form was duly signed and a date agreed for the kitchen fitters to install the £8,000 kitchen. At last, I thought, I was on my way to success.

Alas, a few days later, head office delivered the devastating news the husband had rung in and cancelled the order, despatching my non-returnable £50 down the drain.

Thus, my inglorious career as a salesman came to an end. A career fated never to leave the ground.

*

.

# Chapter Three
## Getting Started as an Investigator

My foray into salesmanship having been an abject failure, I now once again turned my attention to what to do next.

However, this time, I allowed common sense to dictate and I set about putting into practise the premise I had always maintained when advising others on deciding a career: try to choose something that is of a particular interest to oneself, for boredom will then seldom be a factor and the day ahead will be anticipated with enthusiasm and, hopefully, success will invariably follow. Thus, reflection in one's latter years will never bring regret of a working life wasted in tedium.

I recalled a neighbour's son, in my youth, who was academically hopeless and who's parents had despaired for his future. A slight boy and physically weak, he was totally unsuited for the only job he could find on leaving school – tyre-fitting in a busy car repair workshop. Finding the tyres too heavy to lift and the bullying derision of his workmates soul-destroying, he was forced to quit after only a few weeks. He found alternative work in a laundry but the repetitive, boring routine drove him to distraction and he soon left. Before long, he found himself claiming state benefits but this caused such dissent with his parents, who now looked on him as a 'waster' that, eventually, he left home and went into lodgings. Over the following couple of years, he attended night school to pursue his much loved photographic hobby and the last I heard of Jeffery he was a successful wedding photographer.

To be truthful, I had especially enjoyed my previous status as an officer of the law, my years in the CID being of particular satisfaction. But, ruefully, I accepted I was now too old to backtrack.

So I would do the next best thing. I would begin a new career as a Private Investigator. I would utilise the expertise and experience I had gained as policeman; using the telephone, knocking on doors, interviewing people, recording statements and generally conversing with Joe Public. Having always considered myself to be a good 'foot soldier', I was confident I had the determination and tenacity to succeed and the many years spent dealing with the general populace ensured I had sufficient effrontery not to be phased by any rejection I might encounter.

But I knew the road ahead would not be an easy ride. I had no police contacts other than my old buddies in Coventry and Hampshire, I was unfamiliar with the south Wales area and, most importantly, I was not known to the local legal profession from which it was surmised the bulk of the work would probably emanate. Notwithstanding this, once the decision had been made, I immediately set about putting my aspirations into practise.

The first step was to scan the local Yellow Pages and I was encouraged to discover there were more than 100 solicitors listed within the Cardiff area. I went out and bought myself a word processor (household computers had not yet become the norm) and knocked out letters to each and every lawyer in the book, letting it be known I was here and at their bidding. The letters were brazenly emblazoned across the top with the legend 'GB Investigations', a play, of course, on my own name initials and 'Great Britain'.

A visit to the reference section of the city's main library unearthed the Insurance Companies Directory and I sent out similar letters to all suitable companies found in the book.

The lawyers' letters yielded scant response, albeit I did receive a few writs to serve and, over the coming weeks, I began to realise I was going to need more than a reliance on the local legal fraternity to sustain my future requirements.

However, I do have to say that there was one shining light; a certain Mr. Bernard de Maid, a Cardiff solicitor, who did really came up trumps. On receipt of my post, he immediately invited me to his city centre office and although, initially, the resultant work he gave me was not constant, it was the beginning of a professional relationship that was to last throughout the whole of my career as a private investigator. After a while, I became his sole enquiry agent and he was able to supply me with a fairly regular variety of assignments, including accompanying him on occasional prison visits and, sometimes, acting as his 'bagman' in court.

My contact with insurance companies was, likewise, not an imminent success. Without exception, they made clear they were not interested in 'one man bands', but preferred to outsource to organisations capable of handling large volumes of claims. Ever resourceful, I telephoned one company to obtain the details of one of these 'organisations' and, fortuitously, I was pointed in the right direction, Ravenstones, in Manchester, being the recommended agency. A telephone call to its principal, Rod Bond, resulted in an invite to the company's offices in Sale where, eventually, after a training course into the whys and wherefores of insurance claims, I passed muster to be appointed as the agency's South Wales representative. Awarded the illustrious title of Claims Inspector, I was, thereafter, able to enjoy a constant supply of claims to investigate, most of which related to road traffic accidents and vehicle thefts although, sometimes, including others involving personal injuries, as well. Over the following months, having now gained some valuable experience on the road, I followed up advertisements in the Police Review from two similar agencies and, they too, accepted me as their area rep.

Of course, forever mindful of my self-employed status and knowing I would never enjoy the luxury of the financial security of a regular salary, I was still constantly looking at other avenues of supply, regardless of however generous the amount of work I may have had in hand at any given time. But, more on that later.

I was now up and running and well on my way to putting GB Investigations on the map.

*

# Chapter Four

## What does it take?

What does it take to become a private investigator?

Following my many years plying the trade, I feel I am now, in retrospect, amply qualified to expound on the attributes required to make the grade.

Of course, it goes without saying, every one of us has his own peculiar talents and qualities which are unique to that person as an individual and no being on earth has 'everything'. Although, it has to be said, there are certainly many attributes which do lend themselves especially suitable to investigating and the following are but a few.

### Observation and Concentration

Observation and concentration are dependent upon one another and it is rare, indeed, for an investigator to come across evidence merely by chance. Concentration in an observational situation must be constant and deliberate if the minute detail is to be captured. In such instances, it is imperative the mind stays focused, lest a valuable moment to record an incident or take a photograph is lost forever.

On many occasions, whilst engaged in an observation situation, I have found it necessary to follow vehicles. This can be most difficult and certainly not as easy as depicted in films and on

TV where, rather strangely, the only two vehicles on the road are those of the protagonists and, stranger still, the driver of the target vehicle hardly ever notices he is being followed. For the investigator working alone, it can sometimes prove impossible. For example, as it is always wise to ensure there are at least two vehicles between that of the investigator and the followed vehicle, the target is invariably lost as it is driven through an amber light or, perhaps, turns a corner. In the police, where there is practically an unlimited amount of resources, Crime Squads sometimes use up to five or six vehicles, at times even including a motor cycle, when tailing a single quarry. All are in radio contact and when the target vehicle peels off at a motorway junction, for instance, the immediate pursuing vehicle will stay on the motorway whilst one at the rear of the convoy will take over.

The private investigator has no such luxury and the only way to circumvent this problem is to endeavour to discover, prior to the pursuit, the target's eventual destination. Of course, this is not always possible but, on many occasions, the client may suspect, or actually be aware of, where the target is headed and merely wishes for the information to be confirmed.

Following someone on foot also demands particular caution. Eye contact must be avoided at all costs. Once the pursuer has looked the 'prey' in the eye, no matter how inadvertently, the chase is over and he may as well go home. As sure as eggs is eggs, he has been registered - albeit even sub-consciously - and the next time a glance is made in his direction bells will ring.

## Communication Skills

An investigator must be articulate and able to communicate on all levels. On a daily basis, he not only deals with the hoi polloi at the lower echelons of society but also with barristers, doctors and insurance executives and such like. He therefore must have the ability to 'speak down' as well as to 'speak up'. This statement may give the impression of 'elitism' but, whatever one's opinion on this aspect it is, nevertheless, a fact of life. While there are some who have had the benefit of a superior upbringing there are others less fortunate and the investigator must bridge the gap from both directions.

Of equal importance, an investigator must also be capable of producing a precise and to-the-point report, basically articulating the 'who', 'where', 'what' and 'when' salient points in a readable manner. The report must reflect professionalism and its contents must be able to stand up in a court of law, if necessary.

No matter how skilful on the ground the investigator is and how hard he has worked to obtain the requested information, a shoddy report containing spelling mistakes and grammatical errors serves only to convey the impression that its writer is likely to be incapable of dealing with anything other than 'run of the mill' jobs. Thus, the client will obviously be deterred from supplying future work should it be of a more comprehensive nature.

In other words, the investigator is only as good as his written report.

**Perseverance and Patience**

As has already been said, an investigator is paid solely on results and to get these results sometimes means sitting interminably, hour after hour, in a vehicle after perhaps having travelled a great distance to reach the venue. On such occasions, it is imperative he has the patience and perseverance to last the distance to see the job through. It would be utterly futile to succumb to thoughts of home comforts and allow temptation to override professionalism and return to base without completion of the task. That would obviously result in a no-fee situation until the exercise can be repeated at some future date. A total waste of valuable time and effort.

**Discretion and Ability to Keep Secrets**

By the very nature of the profession, an investigator will find himself privy to secrets; secrets divulged to him by his client as well as those discovered during the course of the investigation. It is imperative these are disclosed only on a 'need to know' basis, whatever their source, in order to maintain the investigator's integrity in the eyes of all parties.

If an investigator has trouble in keeping secrets or delights in disclosing tit-bits of information about others to anyone who would lend an ear, he must learn to curb his tongue and refrain from engaging in tittle-tattle. An indiscretion divulged unnecessarily, even to a client, will inevitably diminish trust in the investigator and may even result in future work being withheld on the grounds that he is unable to keep confidences.

Similarly, an investigator must guard against disclosing to the client the source of the information he has obtained on his behalf. The client is paying solely for the information and the information alone and it is most important the source is protected at all costs. The more who are privy to the informant's identity the greater the chances of his exposure, placing risk on his livelihood and even, perhaps, on his very well-being.

## Ability to Obtain Information

Regardless of whatever has been said above, the ability to obtain information is, without doubt, the most important and valuable of the investigator's assets. Without this ability he has no *raison d'etre*.

The would-be investigator must research and cultivate potential informants, depending on whatever avenues of investigating he is choosing to take. The most favourable way to do this, in the beginning, is to network with other, established, investigators, both in his own sphere of activity as well as nationwide.

To this end, it is highly recommended a copy of the "British Directory of Investigators & Process Servers" is purchased, a tome which will, without doubt, prove an invaluable acquisition. This directory lists contact details of companies and sole operatives, based throughout the country, who are able to accomplish virtually any given task or, at least, they can certainly suggest someone who can. Perhaps to serve a writ, take down a statement, take a photograph or even to acquire the most sensitive information imaginable. Putting it rather cynically, anything can be bought if the price is right.

One of my contacts, a Duncan Facer, who lived in Cumberland, was absolutely brilliant at tracing missing persons and, sometimes, details he required to do so often gave clues as to his methods. "Has the missing person ever served in HM Forces? If so, is his service number known?" "Is he in receipt of a State pension?" "Do you know his bank details? Perhaps we can trace his credit card usage." etc.

Once Duncan had delivered me the requested information, discretion dictated I did not need to know his sources and thus, I did not ask. That is how it works.

*

# Chapter Five

## To Tell a Fib

As I reflect on those qualities I have described in the preceding chapters, I am reminded of a particular occasion when they all came into play in one fell swoop.

One Saturday morning, in the 'early days', I found myself sitting in my car in a quiet, residential road located in a little village in West Wales. It was about ten o'clock and, having travelled some 100 miles from base in Cardiff, I had already been there for nearly two hours. It was a bright summer's day. I had my sandwiches, flask and Daily Telegraph and I was prepared for a long wait. The radio was switched on quietly to Classic FM.

There had been virtually no movement in the road, either from its residents or visitors and I felt conspicuously exposed – like the proverbial sore thumb. However, I knew there was no alternative but to patiently sit and wait.

Acting on instructions from a major insurance company, my mandate was to obtain video footage of the resident of one of the neat and tidy bungalows who had apparently been awarded many thousands of pounds in compensation for an injury which had, supposedly, left him totally incapacitated. However, the insurers had now received information to the effect that, not only could he walk perfectly well, but he was actually carrying out some sort of weekend work.

Unfortunately, the anonymous informant had omitted to say where the man was working, what the nature of the work was, or even what day of the weekend it took place. Consequently, on my arrival, I was more than heartened to see the man's car still parked in the driveway of his house. In fact, I was greatly relieved. Had the car not been there, I would have known my whole journey had been wasted and I would have had to return home, rethink my strategy and make another effort at a later date. Without having even covered my fuel costs, it would have been an absolute catastrophe.

That hurdle having been cleared, there was now nothing more to do but to sit it out and hope that it was a Saturday and not a Sunday when the claimant was supposed to be working.

Then, along the pavement came an old man walking his dog. As he reached my car, he crouched down by the driver's window.

"What are you up to?" he asked rather bluntly. "You have been sat here now for a long while. What are you doing here?"

There was nothing unusual in this. I had been expecting it to happen. It is perfectly natural in a good class of residential area for a local to challenge a stranger who has been suspiciously parked up for such a long time. I would do it myself. But, now being on the other side of the fence, I had to have a feasible response. In fact, I thought I had the perfect answer. All my years of experiencing similar situations while carrying out observations in the police had taught me how to tell a plausible fib.

"Oh, my wife and I have always liked this area and we have decided we would like to move here. I have been to that house for sale down the road - the one with the sign outside - to have a look at it, but they are not in. They are probably out shopping and I am waiting for them to come back," I said, pointing to a house in the distance with an estate agent's board outside.

That'll fool him, I thought.

But, his reply wasn't quite what I expected. I obviously wasn't as clever as I thought. "I have never heard such a load of cobblers in all my life. Now, look here, I am a retired police officer and if you tell me what you are up to I might be able to help you. You are looking out for him in number 17, aren't you?"

I now had a decision to make and I had to make it quick. I either had to persist in my fabrication, or else, concede and tell the truth in the hope of getting some useful information from the man. Instinct told me not to do this as I would be giving the whole game away and the assignment would be an irretrievable failure if the decision was the wrong one. After all, the man could well have had some friendly connection with my target and he may have been trying to fool me into giving *him* information.

On the other hand, if he was being honest, he might give me valuable information which could save me a lot of time.

He was looking me straight in the eye, awaiting my reply and I could not afford to be hesitant. Taking the big risk, I decided to grab the bull by the horns, tell the truth and hope against hope he was genuine.

"To be honest, you are right," I said. "I am from an insurance company and I have my eye on that chap who lives over there. I need to know if he is working so I am waiting for him to leave so I can follow him."

"I thought as much," the man said. "Well, I can tell you he works as a disc jockey at the British Legion in the next village on a Saturday night. If you come back at seven o'clock tonight you will catch him just as he leaves the house."

I could not believe my good luck! My gamble had paid off! I was now able to leave and have a ride around the area, suss out the British Legion, have a bite to eat in a pub and then relax with my Telegraph crossword in a quiet spot somewhere until it was time to come back.

Having done just that, I returned at a quarter to seven and, taking up position fifty yards from the target house, I was able to comfortably set up my video camera at just the right angle to get my footage. That was a feat in itself as my camera was not the small, 'palm of the hand' model which is available these days, but an eighteen inch long, heavy and unwieldy contraption that was not the easiest to conceal.

Fifteen minutes later, just as the old man had predicted, the target came out of his house looking fit as a fiddle and carrying a large amplifier which he placed in the boot of his car. A few minutes later, he repeated the trip with another amplifier before retreating back into the house and I was able to get good video shots of both incidents.

Knowing his destination, there was no need to wait and follow him so I was now able to drive straight to the Legion and await his arrival. In the car park, I did some further videoing as he carried the amplifiers from his car into the club.

So far so good, but what I really needed was some footage of him actually performing as a disc jockey. This evidence would obviously negate any claim that, despite being able to carry the equipment, he was still too incapacitated to earn a living.

Giving him about twenty minutes to set up his disco, I went into the premises and introduced myself to the club steward.

Cue for another fib.

"Good evening. I am from Cardiff and my wife has relatives in Chicago whose grandparents originally came from here. They have never been to Wales and they have asked if I could make a video of the village. I have spent most of today filming around the area and this is my last stop. Would you mind if I took some shots inside the club so that they can see what the social life is like here?"

"Not at all," he replied. "No problem. Go where you like."

So I spent the next half hour roaming around the club, pretending to video the bar, the skittle alley and old men playing dominoes, before

23

eventually wandering into the concert hall where the disco was just getting under way. I then got some lovely footage of our man not only doing his bit as a disc jockey but jiving around on the floor, as well.

I later learnt that, after the incriminating tape had been duly passed to the insurance company, legal steps were being taken to recover the original payout from the fraudster.

A job well done with a successful outcome.

And who was the mystery informant who had anonymously telephoned the insurers in the first place? We will never know for sure, but I wouldn't mind betting it was the old man.

*

# Chapter Six

## A Natural Curiosity

We all have a natural curiosity inherent within us; albeit perhaps some more than others.

I have always thought I possessed a particularly persistent trait of curiosity; from my propensity in childhood for dismantling toys to see how they worked to the searching mind of my latter days in studying the characters of my fellow beings. From my curious night explorations of alleyways and back entries in my uniformed police days to my scratchings below the surface as a CID officer when vital evidence needed to be uncovered.

Apart from those qualities discussed in the earlier chapter, I feel a natural curiosity is also an essential attribute an investigator must have.

I would like to share a couple of personal anecdotes which may help to demonstrate the veracity of this assertion.

One day, I dropped in to see my wife's parents, Phyllis and Len, at their home in Cardiff. Phyllis was reading the local paper and she remarked, "George, I have something to show you."

She passed me the paper and pointed to a photograph of an elderly lady in a care home surrounded by friends and relatives. The headline above the picture read, "Care Home Resident

Celebrates 104 Years." The lady was called Mary Rees and the care home was in a nearby suburb.

Phyllis said, "That lady was a customer of mine when I worked in the post office. She must have been in her eighties at that time. I knew her well."

Len said, "I remember her, too. She used to visit my mother when I was a little boy. She was a family friend and I used to call her "Auntie". But I haven't seen her for many years."

I was struck with wonderment. I had never before been so metaphorically close to a person who had reached such an age.

I was intrigued and, after questioning Phyllis and Len a little more, I decided I must take this golden opportunity to meet this lady. I was curious to discover whether she was able to remember her ties with them. After all, the chance of meeting a person who had reached 104 years did not come along every day.

Without telling Phyllis and Len of my intentions, (I was not sure they would have approved of my intended intrusion into the old lady's privacy), I made an excuse to leave and made my way to the care home.

I spoke to the matron on my arrival and, explaining the purpose of my visit, I asked if it was possible to speak to Mrs Rees. I felt it was a delicate issue and, above all, I wanted to be respectful. After all, the lady may not have been in the best of health or perhaps, at such an advanced age, she may not have had the capacity

26

to understand my motives. The last thing I wanted was to selfishly impose myself upon her.

Thankfully, my fears were unfounded. The matron stated Mrs Rees was fully *compos mentis* and that she would welcome a visitor. She guided me to the Day Room and pointed her out, sitting amongst other residents, before introducing me to her.

I sat with Mary (at her instigation, we were soon on first name terms) for only about 15 minutes but, during that short time, I discovered what a beautiful lady she was. We held hands as, bright as a button, she began to reminisce. Although her memory was good, she could not recall either Phyllis or Len, although she did remember his mother.

As I left Mary, I felt uplifted. I had a sense of fulfilment, as if I had traced a long lost friend.

When I returned to Phyllis and Len they could not believe where I had been. They eagerly consumed everything I had to tell them and that, in turn, set them off on their own reminiscings.

A very satisfying afternoon, indeed.

My second story not only illustrates my will to get to the bottom of things but also emphasises the lengths sometimes required to successfully complete an investigation.

Shortly after I retired, I visited an old family friend who had once owned a shop premises located on a busy road not a stone's throw from Cardiff's city centre. He had vacated the shop some 10 years previous to achieve his life-long ambition of becoming an airline pilot.

As I sipped my cup of coffee in his spacious country home in Monmouth, reflecting on the pleasures of my retirement, Gareth came downstairs and said to me, "I have something here, George, which may be of interest to you. It is an old ID card from 1956 which I found in the upstairs storeroom of the shop in Caerphilly Road. I always meant to trace this woman and return it to her but never got around to it. Perhaps you might be interested in giving it a go. It would be lovely for her to have it back."

Was I interested? You bet I was! To return to someone something so personal that had been lost for some 60 years was right up my street. I imagined the joy it would give that person.

Of course, there would be no monetary gain in finding the card's owner but the enormous satisfaction it would give me in returning it to her - if she was still alive and I was fortunate enough to find her - would be profit enough.

I looked at the fresh-faced girl on the photograph and estimated her to be about 12 years old. The Foreign Office stamp on the document showed that the lady would now be about 70. The card was signed by the headmaster of Pembroke Grammar School and it showed the girl's address to be on a road in that town.

The girl's name was Niriam Laventine (that was not the real name on the card but we will call her that for obvious reasons).

Why the card was issued by the Foreign Office and signed by a headmaster, I had not a clue.

Once home, I started digging, and quickly discovered the grammar school to be long gone and the current occupants listed on the Electoral Roll at the address appeared, unsurprisingly, to show no connection whatsoever to the girl. Of course, I surmised that the lady had most probably married in the meantime so, in any case, the surname I was looking at was likely to have been lost in the mists of time.

Normally, in similar cases, my next step would have been to travel to Pembroke and start my enquiries at the house address but, in this instance, as I was doing this enquiry purely for pleasure, I decided to take another route and centre my enquiries round the shop at which the card had been found.

Gareth had already told me the previous owner had been a greengrocer but he was unable to recall his name, so I now considered making enquiries with the Land Registry. But, firstly, I decided to go to the vicinity of the shop and see what could be gleaned from talking to other shopkeepers. Perhaps those of longstanding and well-established businesses might remember the greengrocers name and, perhaps, give some indication as to where I might find him.

At the first one I tried - one of the largest retailers in the road - I hit the jackpot. The owner showed more than a little interest in my quest and immediately recalled the greengrocer had been a Mr Jackman. He also remembered the gentleman had retired to the Rhbwina area of Cardiff. Not only that, but he offered to search his list of clients on the firm's computer to see if he was one of his customers. He explained the database went back many years and that, if Mr Jackman had purchased anything at all in the intervening period, his name and address would be on file.

Unfortunately, the search proved fruitless. Well, not entirely fruitless. A *Mrs* Jackman was found residing in the area in question so I optimistically noted her address and I subsequently found she had a BT telephone listing.

I duly called Mrs Jackman and, although she explained to me the Mr Jackman in question was not a relative or even known personally to her, she did know of him as being the former owner of the greengrocery and, in fact, was aware of the name of the road in which he resided. She did not know the house number but the information she had given me was sufficient to trace him on the Electoral Roll.

Finding Mr Jackman to live at No. 28, I went straight there from the library and an old man in his eighties answered the door. I showed him the ID card and he confirmed he had rented a room above the shop to a woman but, unfortunately he could not recall her name or give any information as to a forwarding address. This was perfectly understandable as she was probably one of numerous tenants who had rented from him and, after all, it was over 20 years ago.

Having drawn a blank with Mr Jackman it was now back to square one.

As a last resort, I decided to enlist the assistance of another investigator, Lynne, a lady with whom I had made friends when I had taken my laptop to her employer for repair. She was not an investigator *per se* but ran her own little sideline as an 'heir hunter', tracing possible heirs to wills.

Like Duncan Facer, Lynne was an outstanding tracer, who used her considerable IT skills to unearth long lost relatives where others had failed and, as I had occasionally given her the benefit of my experience in the past, I was confident she would help me out now in my hour of need.

A week after making contact, Lynne came back to me with an astonishing result. She had found details of a funeral reported in the Pembrokeshire Herald newspaper of a 92 year old lady with the surname of Laventine. The funeral had taken place two years previously and, more incredibly still, Lynne had managed to acquire from the funeral director a list of mourners who had attended the service.

This was a brilliant result. I knew there couldn't be too many Laventines around the Pembroke area, or anywhere else for that matter, so the chances of our Niriam Laventine being a family member were pretty high.

I scrutinised the list of mourners but could not find her name. I was not wholly discouraged by this as I knew she would probably be listed under her married name. But what *was* her married name? That was the problem.

My next step was to telephone around the mourners to try and gather some information but the more common names had to be discounted when making my BT enquiries. It would be no good requesting a number for a Jones, Evans or Smith without an address to go with it. Finding a Rowbotham, I decided the name was uncommon enough to make a start and, luckily, BT had a listing for one in the Tenby area.

A Mrs Rowbotham answered my call and, a few seconds into the conversation, I knew I had struck gold. She told me she was Niriam's cousin and that her name was now Robins. She resided in "a village near Cardiff" but, understandably, she declined to give any further clue as to her actual address. However, she did promise to contact Niriam and pass my details to her and, no doubt, she would call me.

A few days later, my telephone rang and, at last, I had contact with Niriam Levantine.

"Hello. Niriam Robins here. I understand you have my old identity card?"

"Yes. I am a retired private investigator. A friend found the card in his shop in Cardiff and asked me to trace you so you could have it back."

"I will give you my address and you can send it to me."

"I could bring it to you. I would be quite happy to do that. As I said, I am retired now and it would give me something to do."

"No. Just pop it in the post."

The conversation was then terminated and that was it. No thank you or semblance of curiosity as to how she had been traced. Just an enigmatic acceptance and casualness about the whole affair. Perhaps I had expected too much. But I could not help but feel a sense of frustrating anti-climax.

The following day, the card was sent off by recorded delivery. Despite it being accompanied by a few lines on my letterhead, I never received any acknowledgement in return.

As they say up North, "There's nowt so queer as folk."

\*

# Chapter Seven

## Building on Success

I was now getting well established and the work was pouring in from all directions, albeit mostly insurance investigations from Ravenstones and the other agencies. I became so busy that, at one stage, I employed another investigator, a former Met policeman living 30 miles away, to help with the workload. He had recently moved to the area in order to 'downsize', properties being much cheaper in the former Valleys mining areas than those of his home town of Windsor. Having previously worked in the potentially dangerous field of close-guarding celebrities, this would seem to be an ideal opportunity for Cyril; an introduction to a new career and, at the same time, a supplement to his generous police pension.

Cyril had apparently applied to one of my agencies for work but, in view of the fact I already covered his potential areas, they had suggested he give me a speculative call to see if I could assist.

His contact came at a rather fortunate time as I had just taken on a new client who was supplying me with insurance work that required only a telephone conversation with the claimant. Despite being rather time consuming, it was easy work. So easy that, eventually, I was able to type out the claimant's statement directly as it was being dictated. Working from home and involving no travelling, it was money for old rope. A little repetitive, yes, but nevertheless, not complicated for someone like Cyril who was well experienced and competent from his police days in taking statements. It was easy money for a minimum of effort.

After spending a couple of days training him up, I gave Cyril the bulk of this work, meeting him only occasionally at a motorway service area to collect the completed jobs, pay him and hand over his new assignments.

For a while, he turned over the work on a regular basis but then it gradually became clear he was losing his appetite. I began to find it necessary to chase him for jobs for which I, in turn, was being pursued by my client, only to discover that he had become so lax he had allowed a virtually immovable backlog of work to build up. From our conversations on the matter, it became patently obvious he was more interested in his wife's village flower shop and he was just not hungry enough to expend the time and effort required for the insurance work.

As I was now travelling long distances on a daily basis - sometimes as far distant as Birmingham and Devon and occasionally staying overnight - I just did not have the time to keep checking up on him. It soon got to the point where I was in danger of losing this particular client's goodwill, not to mention the steady stream of work he was supplying.

Sadly, I had to inform Cyril I was "letting him go" and we subsequently parted company amicably "by mutual consent".

36

That was the first and only time in my life I had ever employed anyone and the experience - for me, at least - confirmed Napoleon Bonaparte's oft quoted maxim; "If you want a job done well, do it yourself."

The disappointment was such that it discouraged me from seeking to replace Cyril so there was no alternative but to 'lash myself to the mast' and clear the backlog, telephoning the claimants whenever I had a spare hour or so, late evenings. It played havoc with my already meagre social life for a while but, at least, I managed to keep the client

In the wide variety of tasks in which I was involved, I was not always known to the public as a "Private Investigator" and I variously introduced myself in different guises, depending on the job in hand. When representing lawyers, I was a 'Solicitor's Clerk', when I was seeking someone's whereabouts, I was a 'Tracing Agent' and when investigating insurance matters, I was a 'Claims Inspector' and, other times, I was just a plain and simple 'Enquiry Agent'. I felt this necessary as I considered using the word 'investigator' in certain circumstances being somewhat heavy handed and intimidating, especially if the recipient of my call was not specifically suspected of any wrongdoing. As far as the clients were concerned, it did not matter what my title was or what I called myself as long as I did not jeopardise their integrity and was successful in obtaining the requisite information.

I always dressed in the manner in which I wished to be perceived. Consequently, when out in the public domain, I would, invariably, be smartly attired in suit and collar and tie, always endeavouring to reflect my client's ethos. There were, of course, exceptions to this rule, of which I will mention later.

When engaged in the insurance field, I particularly preferred to deal with theft claims as opposed to those concerning accidents. Apart from not enjoying taking road measurements and producing the requisite precisely drawn sketch plans of the scene, there was often difficulty in appointing interviews with the insured persons to obtain their written statements of their versions of the accidents in which they had been involved.

This was because, on receipt of a vehicle-related claim, the insurer's first responsibility is to get the claimant back on the road thus, in accident claims, ensuring the vehicles involved are repaired as soon as possible with the question of liability being resolved at a later date. Hence, in the months following the accident, his car having been repaired, the insured driver was under the false impression the claim has been settled and the incident was now the last thing on his mind. Consequently, the response to my call to arrange the appointment was often something along the lines of, "Oh, that was months ago. That's all finished with now. Everything has been settled." or, simply, "I am too busy. I am a long-distance driver and only home on a Sunday."

I would then have to patiently explain the matter was far from closed, that the two insurance companies were still wrangling over liability and that it was imperative to get his side of the story down in writing otherwise there would a massive increase in his premiums the next time his policy's renewal came around. That usually did the trick. There is nothing like the threat of a financial penalty to ensure co-operation!

Then there was the wonderful variety of explanations on the claim form of how the accident occurred. "The other car came from nowhere." "Suddenly, the bend was right in front of me. I never saw it coming." And, my personal favourite, "You had better ask her. Only she knows what she was doing."

Incredibly, with these brief, ambiguous sentences, the claimant genuinely believed a full explanation had been given on which his insurer could base a liability argument.

Theft claims were a different matter altogether. The person claiming for a stolen vehicle had already received a letter from the insurer advising of my impending contact and he or she was made fully aware at the outset that their claim could not be progressed until they had made my acquaintance. Consequently, they usually fell over backwards to agree to an appointment, even to being available that very day, if so required.

Although my mandate was primarily to establish the veracity of the claim, I was also expected to examine all paperwork relating to the vehicle and highlight any discrepancies. The purpose of this was to afford the insurance company the opportunity to minimise the value of the claim or, at least, establish the vehicle's true value by examining its provenance.

Glass's Car Guide is the universal authority on which insurers base their valuations and the pre-theft condition of the vehicle needs to be known in order to determine which of the three listed values apply. Naturally, in the absence of an unrecovered stolen vehicle, for instance, the only way to determine this is to produce evidence in the form of a paper trail.

Therefore, regardless of which company I was representing, I had a set procedure in place which commenced as soon as the initial chit chat was over and the ice broken. I would ask for all of the vehicle's documentation, including purchase receipt, service history, MOT certificate, driving licence and insurance certificate, and closely examine each and every piece of paper. Occasionally, this gave an insight into whether the claimant had been wholly truthful in his answers in his previous dealings with the insurer or whether, he had sometimes been 'gilding the lily'.

As an example, I would often have to step over old car batteries and worn tyres in the front garden on my way into a scruffy, untidy house located on a sink estate and, when the question arose as to the condition of the stolen vehicle, the response would be something like, "Wonderful. Not a scratch on it. It was my baby. I was always out there cleaning it, wasn't I, Mabel?" Then, on being asked for the service records, "Oh, I didn't bother keeping those."

The 'main user' aspect was often another bone of contention. How many times did I attend to claims where the vehicle was insured in the name of the head of the household but actually belonged to, and was exclusively driven by, his offspring? Incredibly, in the majority of such cases, the parent genuinely believed it to be a legitimate ploy to insure it in his name and when asked why the son or daughter did not have their own policy, I would be looked at in amazement as the innocent reply was blurted out without the slightest hesitation, "Because it's cheaper!"

On other occasions, the middle-aged and staid policyholder would not be so honest and would endeavour to maintain he was the main user. This, despite the fact the stolen vehicle was an SR2 with alloy wheels and, perhaps, other sporty modifications plus the fact there were the same number of other vehicles in the household as there were adult persons.

These were important points to look out for but there were other factors to be also taken into consideration. The insurance companies were not only interested in the documentation and the circumstances surrounding the theft, they also required an opinionated character assessment of the claimant, together with a description of the area in which he resided and the type of house in which he lived. This painted an overall picture to assist them when difficult decisions had to be made.

In practicable terms, the police had little or no interest in investigating thefts of vehicles. Unless the thief had been caught red-handed, which was fairly infrequent, they merely issued the victim with a crime reference number and advised him to inform his insurers. This is still the case today and, of course, as criminals are well aware of this, it only serves to encourage them when deciding to dispose of their own, unwanted, vehicles by devious means and claim on their insurance to compensate for their 'losses'.

In all fairness, no-one has a crystal ball to enlighten them as to whether or not a claim is genuine and, although I often had a 'gut feeling' I was dealing with a fraud, without hard evidence I could only report back accordingly to the insurance company. It was then up to its claims handler to make the decision whether or not the claim was worthy of credence.

*

# Chapter Eight

## Some Case Histories

### *Guns Under the Counter*

Glancing through the claim form, I could see nothing untoward. The claimant was the landlord of a public house and he was claiming for the theft of his motor car, valued at £5,000, which had apparently been stolen overnight from the yard behind the pub, The Penylan Arms, in Merthyr Tydfil.

The fact that the claimant was a licencee allayed any initial suspicions I may have had about the claim. Pub landlords are generally upstanding, honest, members of society who have to endure a legal process to get their licence, appearing before a magistrate after their application has been vetted by the police. Once the licence is granted, it is jealously guarded, its recipient usually going to great pains to keep his nose clean and avoid any infringement of the law which might threaten his livelihood.

Driving along Merthyr's High Street at the appointed time on a Tuesday morning, I was having difficulty in locating the premises until I eventually spotted The Penylan Arms sign above a doorway between two shops. Certainly not the imposing premises I had imagined!

Once inside, I found it to be merely a single bar, a small, poorly furnished room with a few rickety tables and chairs. A solitary customer knocked a few balls around a pool table.

The claimant came from behind the bar and introduced himself. A younger man than I had envisaged, probably in his late twenties, he was dressed in a black T shirt and sported a pony tail. A hail-fellow-well-met type with a big, beaming smile.

We got down to business over a coffee and I began to examine the car's documents. Looking at the VRD (Vehicle Registration Document), I noted from the date of first registration the car was less than three years old, meaning it did not yet require an MOT certificate. I also noted from the change of ownership details that the claimant had owned the vehicle for less than three months.

"Who did you buy the car from? Was it the last keeper?" I asked.

"I don't know. I didn't get his name."

"Where did he live?"

"I don't know that, either. I never went to his house."

"How did you know the car was for sale?"

"I saw it parked on the road one Sunday morning. It had a piece of cardboard on the windscreen with a telephone number. A guy brought it to Tesco's car park later that day."

"How much did you pay for it?"

"£5,000."

"Have you got a receipt?"

"No. I didn't bother getting one."

Alarm bells began to ring. In fact, they were already ringing but now they were getting louder.

Here was a man who, not only buys a car from who knows who, but also does not know where the vendor lives and pays £5,000 without obtaining a receipt. Rather improbable, you might say. But, having previously come across stranger circumstances which had eventually turned out to be genuine, I was careful not to show any reaction. I just blandly carried on, avoiding alerting him to my suspicions and careful not to cause him to be more guarded in his responses. Nevertheless, I was now on my toes, instinct telling me something was not quite right.

"So, you did not get a receipt. Do you have anything else you can give me to show you paid the money? A bank stub from your chequebook, perhaps?"

"No. I paid cash. I always have a stash of cash upstairs."

The pub, even inclusive of all its furnishings, did not look as if it was worth £5,000, so I now knew for definite I would be making further enquiries before my report went in to the insurance company.

But, wait. It gets worse.

As the claimant was signing his name to the written statement he had made regarding the circumstances surrounding the actual theft, a customer came in and asked, "How did you get on in court yesterday?"

"I got remanded to Crown Court," he replied.

My ears pricked up. I asked, "What was all that about? Were you involved in a fight or something?"

"No. Stupid police!" he exclaimed, "I was walking the dog up the mountain late one night after I had locked up and I kicked something in the grass. It was a sawn-off shotgun. I just picked it up, brought it back here, put it under the counter and, from then on, forgot all about it."

He went on, "Then a customer comes in and borrows some money off me. He gives me a pistol and a bullet in a case as surety and I left that under the counter, as well. Then the police raid me for a stolen telly or something - I can't remember now - and now they've got me on firearms offences."

"What bad luck," I said sympathetically, as I closed my briefcase and said cheerio.

Once outside, I made a beeline straight for Merthyr police station. Asking to speak to a CID officer, I was, at first, given the usual brush off by the lady support worker at the counter. That is, until I told her I had highly confidential information for CID ears only. This caused her to spring into action and pick up the phone and, within seconds, a detective sergeant came scurrying down the stairs.

"He's a bad 'un," he said, after I had related my story. "He's into supplying drugs and handling stolen property, amongst other things. He's going down for a long time for the firearms offences."

"What about this stolen vehicle claim?"

"Nothing to do with us, mate. It's an insurance job."

That epitomised the police attitude. They

wanted the evidence on a plate before they would even consider looking at a possible offence. Still, I suppose I was lucky to get someone to talk to me in the first place.

I went home and made a few telephone calls and soon discovered our friend had never owned the vehicle in question. It was a rep's car belonging to IBM, the international computer giant. 'Matey boy' had merely taken its number as it passed by and then telephoned the DVLA and requested the VRD, claiming he had bought the vehicle without the document. Once he had the VRD, he insured the car and then, a couple of months later, submitted a claim for its supposed theft.

It was as simple as that to illegally obtain a VRD in those days. On receipt of the request, the DVLA would merely send correspondence to the true registered keeper, informing them that if confirmation of the change of ownership was not received within 14 days, the VRD would be sent to the 'new keeper'.

The police and insurance companies were well aware of this scam and it was usually quickly forestalled with the minimum of investigation, as had happened in this case. In my report to the insurer, I mentioned the detective sergeant's remarks but, so as not to compromise him, he was given a fictitious name.

And what happened to our would-be claimant?

For the firearms offences, he was sentenced to six months imprisonment which he served at Verne Prison, on the Isle of Portland, in Dorset. I know this because I heard him being interviewed on Radio Wales one day. I was driving in Birmingham at the time and I laughed so much, I nearly crashed the car! Now he was out, he was going to sue the Home Secretary, no less, because the regime in Verne Prison had been so lax. It was, he said, no deterrent at all to potential criminals. He had had booze aplenty, his own key to his cell and – this is the best one – the other prisoners had even taught him how to nick cars!

The postscript to this little story was that, shortly after the radio interview, I was contacted by the South Wales Police Complaints Dept. and asked to attend at its office at Pontypridd police station. On my eventual arrival, the amiable detective chief inspector sat me down with a cup of tea. He told me the 'claimant' had been "stupidly" supplied with a copy of my report by the insurance company in support of its rejection of the claim. He, the claimant, was now making an official complaint against a DS Smith, at Merthyr Tydfil, for releasing the information I was given. The officer now had to be suitably admonished. The problem was, the DCI said, there was no DS Smith at Merthyr or, for that matter, anywhere else in the Force.

"You obviously made a mistake with the officer's name. You can't remember his real name, can you?" the DCI asked, shaking his head from side to side. I, too, shook my head and replied, "Sorry, I can't."

"Thank you very much for your co-operation." he said, as he ushered me out of the door, winking knowingly as he did so.

*

### The Man with One Leg

It was my habit to always arrive early for an appointment. This gave me the opportunity to sit in the car at a quiet spot near to the claimant's house and have a last minute browse through the paperwork to refresh my memory and, perhaps, pick up on something which I had missed the first time around. I could then show I was completely *au fait* with the detail and this, in turn, gave the claimant confidence his insurers were giving his claim due importance.

The case I was investigating today was in respect of a stolen motor car and was peculiar in as much as the underwriter had written across the bottom of the letter of instruction, "NOTE. Claimant has artificial leg."

Nothing else, Just that.

No explanation as to how the man had lost his leg or why he had been indemnified to drive a motor vehicle with such a disability.

To be frank, having not previously investigated a claim in which the insured person had an artificial limb, I was not quite sure what I was to particularly look out for. The claims handler was obviously well aware of it and the underwriters had deemed it appropriate to issue the policy, so what else where they looking for? Why had they considered it necessary to especially append a note to my instructions?

I was soon to find out.

The door of the terraced house was opened by the claimant himself and, as I walked behind him along the corridor towards the drawing room, I noticed he walked quite steadily without any trace of a limp.

I decided to play by ear the artificial leg aspect and mention it only if and when the right moment presented itself.

After being introduced to his wife and mother-in-law, I settled into the easy chair I was offered and got the file from my briefcase. Once the small talk was over, I got down to business and asked to see all of the stolen vehicle's documentation. I put the driving licence to one side for the moment, intending to look at it lastly, immediately before taking the claimant's written statement regarding the theft circumstances.

Everything appeared to be in order. The insurance and MOT certificates were up to date and there was nothing to suggest the VRD was anything other than genuine. The purchase receipt showed that the saloon motor car had been bought from a local dealer some 12 months previously. The insurers had already checked there was no outstanding finance on the vehicle and the clamant produced a full service history. So far, everything was hunky-dory and I was becoming quite impressed with the orderly manner he kept his paperwork.

"Have you any previous claims?" I asked.

"Yes. I have one. I was paid £14,000 for an accident 3 years ago. It was my fault really. I was riding a motor cycle and I turned in front of an oncoming lorry. I lost my left leg."

"You lost your leg?" I said, feigning great surprise. "You have an artificial leg? Well, you would never know, the way you walk"

"Yes," said his wife. "He's wonderful. He can skip and he climbs trees with his grandchildren. When he had it off, he was limping around the ward the next day, showing off to the old ladies."

"Well, that's marvellous," I said, genuinely impressed.

"Yeah, I told them to take it off in the end. I had 9 operations in 12 months and I got fed up. I have been right as rain ever since. I can still do anything I want. I drive a lorry for a living, now"

I then asked to see his driving licence. It was the old style, red docket, photo-less type and, on opening it, I immediately saw a problem looming.

"Was your car specially adapted in any way?" I asked the claimant.

"No. It was just an ordinary car."

"I think we might have a problem here," I said. "It looks like you have been driving without a valid driving licence."

"What? What are you talking about?" he asked, incredulously.

"Look," I said, showing him the licence and reading out the legend that was printed alongside every group, 'SPECIALLY ADAPTED TO SUIT DISABILITY ONLY'.

He stared at the licence and, after a moment's silence, said, "I haven't got any disability. I can do anything you can do."

"Yes, I appreciate that. But, the fact is, you do have an artificial leg and that, in the eyes of the law and the DVLA, takes you into the disabled category," I said, as tactfully as I could.

"I've told you," he replied, raising his voice. "I am not disabled. I can do anything you, or any other man, can do."

I could see that things were now getting serious and he was on the verge of losing his temper. I decided to take the coward's way out; let the matter drop and let the insurance company sort it out.

But, I could not resist one last shot.

"Are you in receipt of any disability benefit?" I asked.

"Of course I am," he replied.

"Why is that, then?" I said.

Utterly frustrated, he raised his voice again, this time to near shouting pitch, "Because I've got a bloody artificial leg, haven't I?"

Thereon, the issue of the artificial limb was not mentioned again and, the situation gradually diffusing as we went along, I continued transcribing the written statement.

At the termination of my visit, the claimant and I tacitly begged not to differ and parted quite amicably.

Subsequent enquiries revealed the claimant's payout was reduced due to his non-compliance with the driving licence conditions.

This tale served to emphasise that not every assignment was as it first appeared, and vigilance was ever required for the unexpected.

\*

### Peek a Boo

I went one day to a notorious housing estate in the Pontypridd area with the intention of obtaining a witness statement from a young lady in support of her mother's injury claim against the local council. It was the usual 'slip and trip' claim, the heel of the mother's shoe having apparently caught in a broken paving slab, causing her to fall to the ground. Taken to hospital by ambulance, she sustained a nasty break to her ankle. She had been accompanied by her daughter.

The injured woman could not be interviewed due to etiquette that decreed the insurer could not interrogate claimants under such circumstances for fear of coercion etc. Her statement of events, together with photographs of the scene, had already been submitted by her solicitor.

There being no contact telephone number available for the mother or the daughter, I was making a speculative, mid-afternoon visit to the young woman's address in the hope of finding her at home.

Parking outside the house and looking across the scruffy front garden, I noticed a bed sheet drawn across the sitting room window, taking the place of the usual drapes.

Repeated knocking on the door for a few minutes did not elicit a reply until I had given up and was halfway back to my car. The door was then opened and, after introducing myself, I was invited indoors. The twenty-something girl, having now identified herself as the claimant's daughter, was more than willing to make the required statement.

Motioning me to an armchair, she took her place on the settee opposite. The body of the settee reached all the way down to the floor, leaving, perhaps, a gap of two or three inches between it and the carpet.

As far as I could gather, the young woman was the only one in the house. There were no sounds of anyone or anything else, neither adult, children nor animals.

Scribbling away on the second page of foolscap, I was some ten minutes into the statement when I heard a slight scraping noise coming from the direction of the settee. I immediately looked up and asked, "What was that?"

"What?" she asked in return.

"That noise. Is there a cat or something under there?"

"No," she replied, "I never heard anything."

It must be me, I thought, and carried on writing.

A few minutes later, it happened again. Only, this time, the scraping was a bit louder.

"Hear that? There it is again," I said.

"No," she said, "I didn't hear anything."

I carried on once again and, once more, the

scrape came. This time it was so loud it was impossible to ignore.

Before I could utter a word, the woman got to her feet, reached down and, with one hand, grabbed the end of the settee and deftly lifted it into the air.

"You had better come out, now," she said.

There, lying face down and flat out on his stomach with his forehead resting on the back of his hands, was a young man.

Crawling out from his hideaway, he said to me, "You won't tell anyone I was here, will you?"

"Nothing to do with me, mate," I replied.

Without another word to either me or the woman, he walked out of the house. I could only surmise he had been avoiding the police or the woman's husband.

The young woman resumed her place on the settee and carried on with the statement as if nothing had happened, without a mention of this bizarre occurrence.

Three days later, I had occasion to visit the same estate to interview a lady whose car had been stolen. Her house was not a stone's throw away from the young woman's. Making small talk, I happened to refer to my previous visit, briefly mentioning the fact that the girl's mother had broken her ankle.

To my amazement, not only was she aware of the incident, but she had actually been present when it had happened.

"Yes. It was terrible," she said. "I was walking right behind them as she stepped on the wet crisp

55

packet and slipped. I helped to pick her up and one of the shopkeepers brought a chair out for her until the ambulance arrived."

"Are you sure she slipped on the packet? I heard her heel got caught in a crack in the pavement," I said.

"No. She definitely slipped on the packet. Someone picked it up afterwards and put it in the litter bin. Everyone around was talking about litter louts. There weren't any cracks in the pavement, as far as I could see."

Enquiring from her as to exactly where the incident had occurred, I noted it was nowhere near the location which the woman's daughter had described.

Unfortunately, the lady declined to make a written statement confirming what she had told me. She did not wish any involvement in the affair and, I have to say, she couldn't be blamed for that. She probably had to spend the rest of her life living on that estate and the fear of repercussions was ample deterrent to make her think twice about co-operating with anyone with the cloak of 'officialdom' about him.

All this was duly reported back to the insurance company, with the result that evidence was later obtained from the Ambulance Service to refute the claimant's assertion as to where the accident had actually occurred.

This was grounds enough for the council to reject the claim.

\*

### The Hungry Parrot

I include this rather comical little tale to illustrate that not all of my jobs were epics but, in fact, could be quite innocuous.

I had a telephone call direct from an underwriter asking me to visit a claimant some 20 miles away, to determine whether he had a parrot. He asked that I visit the address unannounced and make some excuse to surreptitiously gain entry indoors and have a chat with the claimant. I was not to make him aware of the true purpose of my visit although I could inform him I represented his insurers. There would be no paperwork involved; no file and no report - merely a return call to the insurance company with my findings.

The story behind this request was that the man had made a claim for a stolen motor car and had sent his documents to the insurance company. Included was an envelope containing tiny bits of paper with an explanatory note stating they were the remains of the vehicle's MOT certificate. Apparently, the documents had been kept in an open container, a small straw basket, on the top of the Welsh dresser in the kitchen and the claimant's parrot had picked out the certificate from the basket and pecked it to pieces, totally destroying it.

I sat in the spare bedroom at home, the room I had converted into an office and, rifling through some obsolete files, I picked out a few blank forms and filled in the claimant's details. I filled the rest of the empty spaces with gibberish and, tucking the lot into my briefcase, off I went.

Not having being required to make an appointment, I decided a Saturday morning was the most appropriate time to make the visit, speculating the claimant would not be working and, hopefully, he would be at home.

As luck would have it, the middle-aged gentleman who answered the door was, indeed, the man in question. He was most amiable and, on being told I was "looking into" the theft of his car on behalf of his insurers, he immediately invited me in.

We sat at the breakfast table in the sizable kitchen and I explained to the man I had come merely to clarify one or two anomalies the insurers had found on his claim form. From then on, I ad-libbed about police crime reference numbers, local car thieves and the time, date and location of his loss etc.

Suddenly, a huge parrot, a most beautifully coloured bird, flew into the kitchen, swooping and flapping its wings all over the place. It settled on the top of the Welsh dresser.

"It's got out of its cage, has it?" I asked.

"No. She doesn't have a cage. We just let her fly around the house freely. She comes in the kitchen to have a feed. She's a nuisance at times. She has started pecking at my papers I used to keep on top of the dresser so I have to keep them elsewhere, now."

Finishing my cup of tea, I made my excuses and left. The insurance company had its answer.

*

# Chapter Nine

## Writs

**W**rits are a pain.

From time to time, I was commissioned by local solicitors to serve writs and the only good thing that can be said of these assignments was that they did not come around very often. Admittedly, the revenue they generated did help to swell my regular income but, as the fees were fixed, the client could only be invoiced for the actual service of the writ and not for time spent on research and failed attempts. The task was time consuming and rarely was the service of the document achieved at the first attempt. To this day, the situation remains the same.

Firstly, establishing the identity of the person on whom the writ is to be served invariably proves to be onerous. It goes without saying that appointments cannot be made with the target, for the last thing he wants is to be the recipient of a writ. Consequently, he will avoid contact with the server at all costs. Moreover, if he as much as gets a whisper of the writ's existence, he will be on his guard, denying his identity if approached by a stranger and, accordingly, once he is aware of the server's identity, the game is up. From then on, it will be nigh on impossible to pin him down and subterfuge will be called for. There is only one bite of the cherry for the server and, under these circumstances, it is imperative prior enquiries are made to confirm the target's identity for definite.

Even then, the server can run into difficulties for, without a photograph or an admission as to his identity, it is just not possible to be one hundred per cent certain the right person has been collared. All the target has to do is to simply deny his name and, although the server may be sure in his own mind he has the right person, it is not good enough from an evidential aspect. How can he stand up in court and swear he has served the writ on the person named in it when he doesn't know him from Adam?

The one thing in the server's favour is that the writ does not have to be physically accepted by the target for, as long as it touches his person, it is deemed to have been served.

Two cases spring to mind to illustrate these points.

I was assigned to serve a writ on a young man whom we shall call Terry Jones and whose address was given by my client as being on a run-down council estate on the periphery of the city.

The door of the semi-detached house was answered by a middle-aged woman I assumed to be Terry's mother.

"Mrs. Jones? Is Terry in?"

"No. He doesn't live here. He left a few months ago and he only pops in to see me now and then."

"Where is he living now?"

"I don't know. I have never asked him."

"Do you know where he works?"

"No. What do you want him for?"

"Oh, nothing much. A friend is trying to contact him and I thought I would just give a knock as I was passing by. Thanks for your help, anyway."

I returned to the car and drove around for a few minutes to give Mrs Jones the impression I had left the area. She was bound to be watching my departure from the window and I didn't want her to observe my next tactic.

I then returned to the vicinity and parked the car out of sight from the Jones' house and made my way to that of the next-door neighbour.

Pretending I thought it was the target's address, I said to the woman answering my knock.

"Mrs. Jones? Is Terry in?"

"No, love. They live next door."

"Oh, I am sorry. Wrong address. Terry lives there with his parents, does he?"

"Yes, that's right, at least with his mother. The father died some time ago."

"Do you think he might be in at the moment?"

"I don't know, but I doubt it. He's probably at work."

"What time does he come home?"

"I don't know, but he is home most evenings. If you want to catch him for certain, though, I know he sells flags and things in town on a Saturday morning when there's a big rugby match on. He stands at the end of Queen Street."

"I think I will leave it till then. Thank you very much for your help."

I knew the next international rugby game was in 10 days. Without a doubt, Terry would have been informed of my visit that very day so there was ample time for it to slip from his mind in the intervening period. On return to base, I telephoned my client and put him in the picture. It was important to do this as, on this occasion, I was not aware of the writ's contents and they could well have related to something that was imminent. However, I was assured by the solicitor this was not the case and it was in order the service be left in abeyance until the appropriate time.

Mid-morning on the Saturday in question and I arrived at the end of Queen Street in Cardiff city centre. As always on such occasions, a smattering of rugby fans were beginning to gather in the pedestrian areas; out of town early-birds looking forward to a meal and a bit of shopping before the game.

I looked across to where my quarry would be standing. My heart sank! There were 5 of them! All standing in a line in the centre of the wide mouth of the pedestrianised Queen Street, each surrounded by his display of flags, shirts and scarves

Suddenly, it dawned on me what a big, big mistake I had made. I had forgotten to ask the neighbour what Terry Jones looked like. How on earth was I going to know which one was him?

It was no use asking any of the five men which of them was Terry. Like all itinerant vendors, they were paranoid about being identified; Inland Revenue, Council Permit enforcement, Trading

Standards etc. The list was endless and a writ server would obviously be somewhere near the top.

A flash of inspiration suddenly came to my rescue.

I walked behind the line and positioned myself about 10 yards to its rear. Taking a deep breath and in my best parade ground style, I bellowed out at the top of my voice an elongated "TERRRYYY!"

One of the men immediately swung round and, screwing his eyes and craning his neck, he looked into the far distance beyond me for a recognizable face.

He was the only one of the five to flicker and I knew for certain I had my man.

Walking up to him, I thrust the writ into his hands and said, "Terry Jones, is it?"

He replied, "Yes. What's this?"

"Read it and see," I said, and left him in his very obvious state of bewilderment.

The second occasion related to a young lady who was being harassed by her former boyfriend and who had applied through her solicitor to the High Court for a Non-Molestation Order.

The problem was that the man was the father of the girl's newly born baby and he felt he had every right to see his child. Consequently, every day at 6pm, on his way home from work, he would visit the girl in her rented rooms and demand admittance. The flat she occupied was on the first floor of a terraced house and, on his arrival, she would throw the door key down to him from the window. Intimidated and afraid for her safety, she felt compelled to do this as, should she refuse, he would kick the door and shout abuse until he was allowed entry.

To avoid the possibility of immediate repercussions, the girl's solicitor instructed me she should have absolutely no involvement in the service of the writ and it should be executed away from the vicinity of the house.

With this in mind, I went to the man's home address the following evening and the door was answered by a good looking young fellow in his mid-twenties. I was dressed in my usual working attire – collar and tie and suit – with the envelope in my hand.

"Is it Brian Williams?" I asked.

"No. I am his brother. He is not in at the moment."

"What time will he be in?"

"I haven't got a clue. He comes in at all times. He usually has a drink on his way home from work. What do you want him for, anyway?"

"Nothing important," I said. "I'll catch up with him again sometime," and went on my way.

The following day the solicitor called me.

"George," he said. "You know the man you spoke to last night in Habershon Street? It was him - Williams. He pulled the wool over your eyes. The girl rang in this morning and said he went round there later laughing all over his face."

I was fuming. No-one likes to be made a fool of and I was now more determined than ever to nail him.

Explaining to the solicitor the difficulty of the identity aspect, I pointed out that Williams now knew me and this would make the task all that more difficult. Fortunately, he agreed entirely.

"The only thing you can do now, George, is go around to her house when he is due to be there and do your best. There is no big hurry but I would like it done by the end of the week."

Two days later, replete in my gardening gear, wellie boots and baseball cap, I sat in my car in the Grangetown area of the city, waiting for the arrival of clever Mr Williams.

Apart from previously dressing 'to suit the occasion', I had never before had recourse to work in 'disguise', but this was one event which demanded I do so. Williams had met me face to face and knew my intent. There was no way he was going to willingly accept the writ.

Parking my car about 50 yards from the girl's house at the appropriate time, I did not have long to wait. Now *I* had the upper hand – I knew what he looked like but the odds were he would not recognise me, even from a reasonably short distance.

Sure enough, a car stopped near to the house and the driver alighted. Straightaway, I recognised him as the man I had seen in Habershon Street.

I waited until he had reached the garden gate before I got from my car. As he walked down the path towards the door, I shambled along with my head down, trying to time my pace to reach the gate at the same time as the girl threw down the key.

It worked perfectly. I went through the gate just as Williams was opening the door and, as he had his back to me, I was able to run down the path and reach him just as he stepped inside and was about to close it. My rubber-soled 'wellies' ensured my approach went unheard. Once inside the house, he turned towards me and, suddenly realising what was happening, tried to close the door in my face. As he did so, I quickly threw the writ through the gap. It hit him on the upper arm before dropping to the floor.

The door swung open and, picking up the writ, he threw it back out. "It missed, you punk," he said.

I replied, "It's served," and walked away, leaving the document on the ground.

The unsavoury aspect of all this was that the girl's well-being may have been put in jeopardy, the domestic issues between her and the father of her child being exacerbated by the service of the writ.

Unfortunately, my hands were tied in this respect. Acting under the solicitor's guidance, I could only do my best in the prevailing circumstances to achieve, what was for me, at least, a successful outcome.

As I said in the beginning, writs are a pain.

*

# Chapter Ten

## The Child Migrants Trust

Tuned to Radio 4 in my car one day in the late 1990s, my attention became transfixed by the story being told by an elderly man with an Australian accent. He was explaining how, as a child of 10 years, he had been sent from a children's home in England to Australia's outback to work on a farm. He had stayed in Oz ever since and this was the first time he had returned to the country of his birth. He had been dispatched 'down under' without being asked, without a chance to say goodbye to his family and without pity or compassion. Over the ensuing years, he had been physically abused and, as a child, had received no remuneration for his labour, apart from food, clothing and lodging. He had now come back 'home' in an effort to find any member of his family who might, by chance, still be alive.

I was listening to a programme about an organisation called The Child Migrations Trust, based in Nottingham, which had been set up to assist such returnee migrants in their efforts to find their lost next of kin.

These innocent children, all inmates of Children's Homes, had been victims of a supposedly enlightened government scheme dreamt up by some anonymous civil servant with the intention of giving them a better start in life. The authorities at the time had, no doubt, been well intentioned but the plan had been a spectacular disaster and its initiators had blindly refused to admit their incompetence and bring the children back.

I listened as the old man's harrowing story was repeated time and time again by other people, both male and female, all now in the latter years of their life, who had been sent, variously, to Australia, Canada, and New Zealand, by the British Government, in the years after the War. As they grew older, despite their repeated pleas, they had been denied any information in relation to their families, being told their blood relatives were either long dead or else they did not wish to be contacted. They had now returned to the UK to find out for themselves and were being assisted in their quest by The Child Migrants Trust.

I had a particular interest in these stories as, despite not having previously heard of the Trust, I had, in the past, personally met someone who had a strong connection to one of these unfortunate souls.

My wife and I had attended a social function and offered to give an elderly lady a lift home. During the journey, she told us how her single parent mother had found it hard to cope with her children and had placed her and her 10 years old sister into the care of nuns in a local children's home. She was 13 at the time and it was meant only to be a temporary arrangement until her mother got back on her feet. However, within a few months, a man had visited the home and extolled the virtues of living in Australia and explained that he had come to choose some children to be sent there and her sister was one of those selected. Their mother had been informed and, apparently, had consented.

The old lady described how she had been taken to the railway station to see her little sister onto the train. The child had clung to her on the platform and cried but a nun had torn them apart and said, "There, you don't have a sister now."

Within a short time, their mother had died and, for many years after, the lady had tried and tried again to get information from 'the authorities' as to her sister's whereabouts but she had been blocked at every turn and, eventually, she had to give up.

Fortunately, there is a happy ending to this tale. 30 years after being sent away, the sister turned up on the lady's doorstep with her husband and two children. Following the joyful reunion, they remained in close contact and she has since visited them in Australia on several occasions.

After listening to the radio programme, I took the trouble of contacting The Child Migrants Trust to offer my services to assist in tracing the relatives of those concerned. I was promised a call back.

I was able to take this step because I had recently come into possession of a disc containing the Electoral Roll for the whole of the UK and it would have been a fairly easy task to trace a whole host of the missing relatives. It was an excellent tool; at the touch of a button and a few seconds on the keyboard, a search engine brought up all the relevant names and addresses.

I made the Trust aware of this, but sadly, despite emphasising I was offering my services free of any charge, the promised call back never came.

I had acquired the disc for a pittance from a BT engineer contact. The same disc, or one which does a similar job, is now widely advertised on the internet and is available to anyone willing to pay the few hundred pounds cost, albeit it does need replacing every twelve months in order to keep pace with the updating of the Electoral Roll.

The disc would have been an absolute boon to me had it been available in those earlier years when tracing people was a major part of my operation. All the hours spent in public libraries would then have been eliminated or, at least, minutely minimised, by that mere touch of that magic button in my back bedroom office!

*

# Chapter Eleven

## Tracing

On the subject of tracing; in 1996, long before the disc came into my possession, I walked into the head offices of the local electricity board which supplied power to the whole of South Wales. I figured it must have a debt collection department and, although I was not interested in any involvement in the actual collection of revenue, common sense told me the company must have an interest in tracing absconders, e.g. consumers who had moved house, owing the company money without having left a forwarding address.

And so it proved. My enquiry led to an introduction to the Debt Manager and I soon sold her the concept of engaging me to trace some of the company's many absconders. Surprisingly, this appeared to be a new idea which, seemingly, had not entered her head.

I was given a batch of hand-written pieces of notepaper, each containing the name and last address of the absconder and off I went on my travels to try and locate the missing defaulters.

These enquiries would fit in neatly with the other work I had in hand and, as I travelled around the country, this was obviously good management of my time as well as a saving on fuel costs. At the time, I did not have a home computer but completed my paperwork and insurance reports on my word processor and, consequently, I did not have access to the internet, which, in any case, was still in its infancy. This meant the tracing aspect entailed a lot of legwork. Every address had to be visited and the current householder spoken to. If that failed, the next step was to talk to neighbours and, sometimes, even the corner shop. I went wherever the enquiry took me until, armed with some clues, I would visit the local library and search the Electoral Roll, street by street, in the area in which I was interested. As they were the only places where the registers were kept, I spent many hours in libraries up and down the country, in quiet solitude, poring over page after page, until a name finally caught my eye.

Sadly, this wonderful facility no longer exists, despite authority's denials to the contrary. Since the inception of the Electoral Roll in 1832, it has been the public's absolute right to examine the register without hindrance and, for this purpose it has, until recently, been available in every public library in the UK. Now, the Roll has been removed from all libraries and enquiries appertaining to the register have to be made by telephone to local council offices. No longer can a member of the public browse the register at his will in privacy, but he must now declare the address in which his interest lies and, in return, the authority will merely confirm the names of its occupants. A request for a random name search on the register is not acceptable, thus nullifying what was once a vital tool in the investigator's armoury. This is not merely a cost cutting exercise, as is claimed, but yet another bureaucratic ploy engineered to further deny the general populace its freedom of information.

But, back to my tracing. Thankfully, due to the electricity company's apathy, many of the traces I was given were pretty old. This was to my advantage as, the longer the subject had been missing, the easier he or she could be traced. This was because ample time had elapsed in the intervening period for the person to be updated on the Electoral Roll at his or her new address. (This still applies today and it is worth noting there are far more registers currently in the public domain on which the majority of us are listed than hitherto. I read recently of one London tracing agency which has access to no less than fourteen such systems.)

Of course, it also goes without saying that the more unusual the name the easier it is to trace. For example, there are a multitude of Jones, Morgans and Smiths listed on public registers but rather fewer Izwoskis.

At the end of every month, I would take the completed sheets of notepaper back to the electricity company, complete with the new addresses of those I had traced written on the back – but not before I had photocopied them to maintain my own personal record of absconders. The company paid me for successful traces only and as I eventually became quite accomplished at locating the absconders, the assignment became a 'nice little earner.' However, I could not help but think that with all their resources, there must be a much easier way for the electricity board to trace their debtors and, of course, there was. And the answer was really quite simple.

After about three months, I said to the debts manager, "Jill, I might be doing myself a disfavour but why don't you just trace some of these people on your computer? After all, unless they have moved from Wales, they are likely to be on a new supply somewhere with your company. You only have to match their names up with dates of new consumers and there you have your absconders, or some of them, at least."

She replied, "This department does not have a computer."

The building in which her office was located was massive and there were, quite literally, dozens of other offices on the premises.

"Well, use one of the other departments' computers."

"I am not allowed to. Each department has its own budget and I would be using another manager's staff and facilities."

I was, at first, flabbergasted. But, that was the moment I came to realise that the electricity company, as an entity, with its millions of customers, was not really interested in employing 'doing what it takes' tactics in tracing their absconders. In other words, there was no sense of urgency or determination. It was merely paying lip service to the cause and scratching its surface. As long as the bosses with their big salaries could face the shareholders at the AGM and point out their debt recovery rate had risen in the past twelve months, albeit by a micro percentage, everyone would go home happy. No-one ever lost their job for incompetence and the world carried on turning just as it had before.

However, I have to admit the company did eventually drag itself into the 21$^{st}$ century. After some three years as its exclusive 'tracer', I was summoned one day to the debt office to be informed by Jill my services were no longer required. She had now engaged a large organisation, "with computer systems," to carry out the work in my stead and my services had come to their natural conclusion.

Although I had, at that time, plenty of work pending from other sources, I left the electricity company not only with dejection, but with frustration, too, as I knew had been doing an excellent job.

Back at my office, I looked at the file containing the new addresses of some 200 electricity absconders I had traced over the time and wondered to what use I could put them. I soon came up with what I thought might well be the perfect answer. I would canvas the gas board and offer the list to them. On the same terms as the electricity company, of course. I surmised that anyone who had moved address without paying their last electricity bill was, more than likely, to have done the same in relation to their gas supply. Surely the gas board would be absolutely delighted for someone to present them with new addresses for 200 of its absconders?

I was soon to be disillusioned.

On calling the Debt Manager at the gas company's local office and outlining what I had been doing for the electricity board for the past three years, I put the offer on the table. Could we, perhaps, come to some arrangement?

"Not interested", was his curt reply, before going on to expound about Data Protection and the "immorality" of using information which had been gathered on behalf of another organisation.

In short, a 'brush-off' from a salary-secure fat cat, spouting off about ethics instead of considering a very real opportunity of recovering his employer's - and its shareholder's - lost revenue.

*

# Chapter Twelve

## Undercover

As with all self-employed disciplines, there were occasional slack periods when assignments seemed to arrive only in dribs and drabs. Every industry in which the protagonist operates independently suffers from this syndrome; from plasterers, plumbers and bricklayers to salesmen and financial advisers, incoming work is never guaranteed to be wholly constant.

During one of these periods, I responded to an advertisement in the Police Review from a company looking for investigators to carry out undercover work. This rather appealed to me and, intrigued by its obvious mystique; I saw it as an opportunity to improve my repertoire as well as gaining an insight into another aspect of my profession.

Taking a day off, I travelled up to Birmingham for the interview with Sanderlings Solutions and discovered that the company specialised in loss management on behalf of national retailers, including a certain builders supplier. It operated by placing 'moles' in the yards or behind the counters of the retailer's warehouse outlets; operatives who would report back on any staff wrongdoing they observed. The job necessitated spending several weeks - ostensibly as a new employee - working on the premises and gaining the confidence of the 'old hands' to the point where they were totally relaxed and comfortable in the mole's presence.

I was given to understand Sanderlings Solutions was a massive organisation which had offices in various parts of the country and conducted operations throughout the whole of the UK. Its activities were diverse and ranged from 'mystery shopping' on behalf of large departmental stores to recovering tool hire equipment and investigating the theft of plant hire.

From what I learnt, it seemed there would be plenty of scope for future advancement within the organisation should I have the good fortune to secure a position with the company.

I was interviewed by Mr Sanderlings himself. Mr Richard 'Dickie' Sanderlings, to be precise. He was a former detective inspector in the West Midlands Police and, being a former detective myself from the same Force, we had much to talk about – mutual acquaintances etc – and we got on rather well. My background and experience seemingly OK, he agreed to take me on, although still on a free-lance basis. The remuneration would include a monthly pay cheque from the client company as well as an equal amount from Sanderling Solutions and I would, therefore, be receiving what amounted to double wages. I would also be travelling to the south coast and staying in a five star hotel, together with the other company members engaged in the operation.

At first, the package appeared to be too good to turn down but, realising I would be away from my base for six days a week for an indefinite period, I was reluctant to commit myself to what would amount to a complete loss of independence. I feared for the client base I had built up over the years - a relinquishing of the goodwill and generally steady income I was already enjoying.

On discussing these misgivings with Mr Sanderling, I found him to be most understanding and sympathetic and, after some consideration, he offered a far more flexible option. Would I care to join one of the company's travelling undercover teams? Each team consisted of two or three men, posing as builders, whose task was to test the integrity of the merchant's drivers by ordering materials and engaging the drivers in conversation as the deliveries were unloaded on site. The pay would be the same, albeit it would be only for the days worked - which seemed fair enough - and I would be required only two or three days a week. I could either travel on a daily basis with fuel costs paid or else enjoy the overnight hotel stays, still at the company's expense. I would then be able to catch up on my 'normal' assignments from my home base on the remaining days. Would that be more suitable for me? I quickly decided it certainly would and travelled home that day happy and confident in the knowledge that, at least in the short term future, I was going to be making some good money. This would obviously sustain me through the current quiet period until my regular work got back on track.

Having cleared up my few outstanding commitments over the following weekend, I joined up with the team, somewhere on the outskirts of Bournemouth, on the following Monday morning.

On my arrival at the rendezvous, I found the address I had been given to be an empty bungalow situated in a quiet residential road. I had left base some three hours earlier, attired as a typical 'workie' in his uniform of jeans, boots, old sports jacket and flat cap. Oh, and I hadn't bothered to shave, either.

The 'team' were sitting outside the house in a hired van. There were just two of them, "John" and "Sean", and, after our initial introductions, we discussed our respective backgrounds. John was a former sergeant in the Military Police and Sean was an ex-Surrey policeman. We spoke the same language and, pleasingly, we gelled straightaway. This was essential if we were to live and work together, albeit for only intermittent periods.

Both John and Sean had apparently been engaged in this work for the company for some time and, as they were obviously well experienced, I decided there and then to merely fall in behind and allow myself to be guided and advised by them.

John was clearly the man in charge. I immediately recognised his dominant personality and could see he was a very capable character. His leadership qualities shone out and I felt I would be quite comfortable in following his lead.

Prior to my arrival, they had already visited one of the client's builders' depots and ordered a few bags of sand and cement and we were now awaiting delivery.

The bungalow, on which we were supposedly carrying out renovations, had a large 'For Sale' sign planted at the end of the driveway. It had been picked at random by the other two whilst driving around the area, for the sole purpose of providing a delivery address.

We waited in the van, backed into the drive, for about an hour until the delivery lorry turned up and stopped nearby.

John got out and spoke to the driver, a fellow in his forties, "Hello, mate. Just drop the bags there. We'll probably see you again as we are here for a couple of weeks."

The lorry drove off and John explained how, over the coming weeks, we would be ordering more deliveries and developing a rapport with the driver. More than likely, it would be the same driver every time as the road in which the bungalow was located was probably on his regular delivery route.

As soon as the wagon left, we loaded the bags of sand and cement into the back of the van. We then set off deep into the countryside where we eventually pulled into the drive of an imposing residence. This was the home of one of the client's directors and, after humping the bags into the spacious garage at the side of the house, we then set off again to make our way to a different area, some fifteen miles away, to scout around for

81

a second vacant property and repeat the exercise with a driver from another depot. This time, John made the order from a telephone box, using a special order number to pay cash on delivery.

Over the ensuing weeks, we were to carry out this routine over and over again.

Apparently, all the materials accumulated during our devious activities would be stored in the director's garage until the end of the operation, when arrangements would be made to have them returned to the depots from which they originated.

Right from the beginning, despite my confidence in John's leadership, I became more than a little uneasy with the nature of the operation. During our conversations, it became clear that our task was to groom the drivers and inveigle them into stealing from their employers. I did not like this at all. It smelled too much of *agent provocateur*. It was one thing to catch someone stealing but to entice him to do so was quite another matter.

On mentioning this to John, he was quite blasé and quoted all the reasons why our methods were justified. "The drivers are all over 21 and know what they are doing", "No-one is twisting their arms", "If they are honest they won't do it", "They are probably "well at it", anyway", etc etc. I allowed myself to be convinced by this reasoning and, thenceforth, carried on regardless.

However, to salve my conscience, I can say, hand on heart, that during the six weeks the three of us worked together, I was not once called upon to actually speak to a driver other than to make light conversation or pass the time of day during the unloading of the materials. On every occasion, it was John who took the lead and began the nurturing process and furthered it to the end when, eventually, stolen goods would often be delivered to us and cash would be handed over in lieu.

Sometimes it worked and sometimes it didn't. Some drivers succumbed and some resisted. All I can say is that, on the whole, it was a successful operation with numerous drivers allowing themselves to be drawn into the net.

One day, John received a telephone call from Sanderlings to the effect that the operation was over and we could all go home. He was to submit a report from which the drivers' fate would subsequently be decided. No doubt, dismissals would follow.

For me, personally, it was somewhat of a relief to receive this information. I had never been completely satisfied with the ethics of the methods we had been using to entrap the drivers and I could now look forward to returning to what I considered to be my 'proper' investigative work. Coincidently, that very day, I had had a conversation with one of the miscreant drivers which had further troubled my conscience.

Bill was over 6 feet tall. A straight and upright man, whose full head of dark hair and generally handsome appearance belied his 60 something years. He appeared to be a little deaf and when I tactfully questioned this, he told me he had been a teenaged Grenadier Guardsman serving on the front line during the War. He had been captured but had escaped from the POW camp. Following his recapture, he had been interrogated by the Gestapo who, by way of punishment, had fired a pistol next to his right ear, causing permanent damage to his eardrum.

I felt humble with pangs of shame. Here was a man who was a true war hero, a man who had served his country well and who stoically accepted the brutality of his injury without complaint. A man who was about to lose his livelihood on the cusp of his retirement. And here was I; a man who must share the blame for that; a man who would never be half the man *he* was.

I went home with the feeling that, financially, it had been well worth my while but not an episode of which I could be particularly proud.

*

# Chapter Thirteen

## For the Sake of a Telly

In 1997, I was tasked by a national TV rental company to investigate various suspected thefts of its televisions and video recorders. These were cases in which the hirer of the equipment had either absconded or else had failed to make any rental payments apart from the initial installation fee.

In the latter instances, the defaulted hire agreements were at least 12 months old, during which time the local depots managing the rentals had abandoned all efforts to collect the outstanding weekly payments. Likewise, the recovery of the equipment having been equally disregarded, those hirers who lacked any intention of paying from the word go (which was the majority) had been left with the distinct impression their withholding of the televisions and video recorders had been successful. As far as they were concerned, they could now treat the equipment as their own.

From the outset, I could see the recovery failure was, more often than not, due to the employees' lack of tenacity and commitment. It was the same old story. Cushioned in their salaried positions and buoyed by job security, those responsible would make only half-hearted, token efforts before prematurely 'writing off' the equipment. This was done after only three visits had been made to the defaulter's address when either no reply had been received or else the hirer had even made a downright refusal to allow the equipment to be collected. Working earlier than 8am or later than 6pm was alien to these "debt reps", which meant the target addresses were never visited at the times when the hirers were most vulnerable. In other words, they simply did not do what it took to get the job done.

I had placed an advertisement in the local paper as a result of which I was approached by the company. I had always held the opinion that one could have the best product in the world but if it was not 'shop-windowed' it was useless since no-one knew of its existence. Luckily, the advert had been spotted by a regional manager who had referred it to the company's head office in Bedfordshire.

Following the usual interview process, I was hired on a non-contractual basis to cover the whole of the South Wales and West of England areas and was to be paid on the basis of each item of equipment recovered plus my expenses. As I was still able to continue with my other investigating activities at the same time, this commission turned out to be a most rewarding venture and the debt reps' lack of diligence simply proved to be my gain.

But I soon discovered that wresting the television or video from the hirer's grasp was not as easy as I thought. At times, I was no less than astonished at the lengths some of these people would go to and the excuses they would concoct merely to hang on to a television. Such was their reluctance to part with it, they would resort to downright lies, even to denying the existence of their own children, as will be seen later.

One of my early efforts at recovery was on a bright, sunny Saturday morning when I drove to a tiny village up a Welsh valley with the intention of retrieving a small, 18" television set. There was nothing unusual written on the note pinned to the original copy of the contract, merely confirmation that not a single payment had been made in the 13 months since the set had been installed.

I found the address to be on a very modern 'council' estate, the houses being flat roofed and neatly painted in white. A knock on the front door was answered with the opening of the elongated bathroom window immediately above my head. A young woman's face peered out.

"Yes, who is it?"

Looking up, I asked, "Mrs Williams?"

"Who is it? Who wants to know?"

Flashing my Alpha TV Rentals identity card, I replied, "I've come to collect the telly."

"Mrs Williams isn't in at the moment. I'm just baby-sitting," she said.

"What time will she be back?"

"Probably in a couple of hours. They are out shopping in Caerphilly."

"Ok. I will come back later."

Looking at my watch and seeing it was only 10 o'clock, I decided to sit on a nearby bench, bask in the sunshine, and read my paper to await the return of Mrs Williams.

87

The house was in full view of the bench, which was very pleasantly situated on a hillside overlooking the wooded area that had once been the site of the local coal mine. An old man was seated at one end and I sat at the other. He had obviously observed my encounter with the woman.

I had no sooner settled and unfolded my paper when he said to me, "Who are you looking for, mate?"

"Mrs Williams," I replied.

"That was her you spoke to," he said.

"You're joking," I replied.

"No, I'm not. I live next door. That was her you spoke to."

"Thanks," I said and walked back to the house and again knocked on the door. No reply.

I knocked repeatedly for several minutes and, still, no-one came.

I was now more resolute than ever the woman was not going to get the better of me. There is nothing more guaranteed to increase my determination than someone trying to dupe me and this was one of those occasions.

I turned my back to the door and started kicking it forcefully with the heel of my shoe. This not only made a louder noise than my knuckle-knocking but also had the door shuddering on its hinges.

But, despite my incessant kicking, there was still no response and I finally had to admit defeat and walk away.

However, I had hardly reached the garden gate when the door was suddenly flung open. A young man dressed only in his underpants and trainers ran towards me and thrust his face aggressively into mine.

"What the f*** do you want?" he shouted, his eyes popping out of his head.

Not budging an inch, I calmly stood my ground.

"I've come to collect the telly," I said.

Fully expecting a prolonged confrontation, you could have knocked me down with a feather when he then shouted, "Then get in there and get it."

Needing no further encouragement, I was in the house like a shot. Going straight into the living room, I spotted the TV on top of a chest of drawers. Mrs Williams was sitting nearby, weeping into a tissue.

Ignoring her, I went to take down the two or three birthday cards that were standing on top of the set.

At this, she jumped from her seat and screamed, "Get your hands off those cards! Don't you dare touch my baby's cards!"

Brushing past me, she grabbed the cards and ran from the room.

Carrying the little telly back to my car, I could not help but wonder at the tiny minds some people must have and the dull lives they must lead when a television means so much to them.

Of course, all these TVs were the conventional cathode tube sets, forerunners of the modern flat screens. The larger sized models were especially weighty, unwieldy and awkward to carry.

On another occasion, this time on a Saturday afternoon, I went to collect a 42 inch model and, on driving into the suburban estate, I found vehicular access could only be gained along the lane at the rear of the terraced rows of houses. This suited me fine as I surmised I would park directly outside the hirer's back gate, carry the telly out of the kitchen door and down the short garden path before humping it into the boot of the car. Unfortunately, I found the tall, wooden gate to be bolted and there was no way I could attract the householder's attention to come out and open it. I had no alternative but to leave the car parked there, walk the 100 yards to the top of the terrace, around the end of the block, and traipse another 100 yards down to the front door of the house.

As I walked down the central pavement running between the gardens, I could now see the houses were 'back-to-front', the kitchens facing onto the front gardens with the lounge areas obviously being at the rear.

The door was answered by a pleasant, middle-aged lady who identified herself as the hirer. She agreed immediately to the recovery of the television, the conversation being short and sweet, it went something like this.

"Good afternoon. Mrs Baldwin? I'm from Alpha TV Rentals. I've come to collect the television."

"It's in there," she said, nodding towards the front room. Without further comment or without even lifting her head, she nonchalantly carried on washing the dishes at the sink, as if it was an everyday occurrence for a repossession man to walk into the house and go about his business.

Amazed at my good luck, I couldn't get to the lounge quick enough.

But my elation was short-lived when, on walking into the room, I was met with the sight of three burly men sat on pouffes in front of the television, chins resting on their hands, intently engrossed in The Open, with Tiger Woods just about to take a swing.

Hiding my apprehension, I made directly to the back of the set, pulled the plug from the socket and began to wind up the lead.

The three men looked at each other, speechless in stunned amazement.

Anxious to get out before they awoke to what was happening, I picked up the heavy set and staggered into the hallway.

On reaching the back entrance, I carefully lowered the television to the floor to leave my hands free to open the door.

Mrs Baldwin suddenly emerged from the kitchen and came to life.

"Where do you think you are going with that?" You are not taking it out that way. You can go out the way you came in."

"But my car is out the back," I protested.

"I don't care. You are not going out that way."

With that, she opened the front door and stood with her arms folded until I had picked up the set again and struggled out into the front garden.

How I made it back to my car without dropping the telly, I will never know. Of course, I *was* in my prime in those days!

It was sheer spite on Mrs Baldwin's part and, obviously, her revenge for the humiliation of having her television repossessed.

At least she was honest enough not to deny she had never had the equipment; unlike the numerous hirers I came across who often went to devious lengths to put me off the scent. One such instance immediately springs to mind and also emphasises the point I made earlier in relation to tracing people with unusual names.

A young lady from Swansea by the name of Lorna Saporiti had disappeared from the rented accommodation in which a television and video recorder had been installed, taking the two pieces of equipment with her.

Not having any joy from the present occupiers of her last address (apart from learning Lorna's boyfriend was serving time in prison), I sat down with the Electoral Roll in the city's main library and went methodically through virtually the whole of the city, from one road to the next. An hour later, I came across a family of Saporitis residing in what I knew to be a particularly good class of residential area. Lorna was not listed at the address but I surmised that, with such an unusual name, the occupiers were likely to be members of her extended family.

The detached house proved to be a very well appointed property, with neat hedging and trimmed lawns etc. The door was answered by an elegantly dressed, middle-aged lady. A young man stood at her shoulder.

"Good afternoon. Mrs Saporiti? Is Lorna in, please?"

"Who? Who is Lorna?"

"I am trying to contact a young lady called Lorna Saporiti. I thought she might live here or perhaps you could tell me where I might find her."

"I have never heard of her," the woman answered with a puzzled frown. Turning to the young man, she said, "Have you heard of her?"

"No," he replied.

"What do you want her for?" the woman asked.

Working on the premise that, sometimes, you have to give a bit of info to get some in return, I replied, "Oh, nothing much. She rented a telly some time ago and they are looking to get it back. Actually, I think the rental company just want to write to her about it. I am just a friend of someone who works in one of their shops and she asked me to pop by on my way home."

"Well, if you leave your telephone number I will ask around and see if anyone knows her. If I find out anything I will give you a ring," she answered.

Quite evidently, my clever assumptions had failed to work this time although I still had the gut feeling that Mrs Saporiti was, in some way, connected to Lorna. It seemed too much of a coincidence they both had the same unusual surname. However, if she chose not to admit it, there was nothing further I could do.

I gave her my card, but feeling it was a charade and that I would most probably never hear from her.

"Sorry I can't help you further," she said, closing the door.

Despite being convinced I was probably on the right track I knew that, in reality, I was back where I started.

As a last resort and knowing Lorna had a connection with the local constabulary through her boy friend, I decided to give the police a try.

Scurrying straight down to the main police station in the city centre, I asked the uniformed officer behind the counter if I could speak to a CID officer. To my very pleasant surprise, I was not then subjected to the usual interrogation following such a request, the officer merely picking up the phone and dialling a number before passing the handset to me.

This was a long shot. I was well aware CID officers generally did not take kindly to being dragged downstairs without good reason to talk to misinformed members of the public who, more than likely, wanted to discuss something which could be adequately dealt with at the front desk.

A young man's voice came over the line and, with a little added embellishment here and there I, more or less, told him the truth. I told him I was the company's head of security and was seeking a young lady called Lorna Saporiti to question her regarding her involvement in a possible case of fraud. I needed to contact her to "clear up one or two things" before officially reporting the matter to the police. He wouldn't know where I could find her, would he?

The officer came downstairs a few minutes later clutching a brown folder under his arm and invited me into a side room. We sat down facing each other over the table and I filled him in with the details, embroidering them slightly, here and there.

"As a matter of fact, I do know the lady and where she is living but you do appreciate I cannot give out that information?" the officer said.

"Of course," I replied, "I was just wondering if you could point me in the right direction."

After a few more minutes of small talk, he looked at his watch and said, "Would you excuse me? I have to make a quick phone call. I will be back in a 'sec'."

With that, he got up and left the room, leaving the unopened folder on the table. I quickly opened it and looked inside. There, on a solitary slip of scrap paper, was scrawled, "Lorna Saporiti", with an address written below. Committing the details to memory, I closed the folder and sat back and twiddled my thumbs, whistling a happy tune to myself.

The young detective came back in, picked up the folder, and said, "I am sorry I can't help you any further but, good luck."

Thanking him for his time, I shook his hand, and left. As I did so, I could not help but muse on that old saying, "If you don't buy a ticket, you can't win the lottery."

It was mid-afternoon, school leaving time, when I drove into Lorna's road and a few mothers were bustling along the pavement on their way to collect their children.

On stopping outside the address I had filched from the folder, I made to get out of the car. As I did so, who should emerge from the front door of the house, manoeuvring a pushchair? None other than Mrs Saporiti, the woman I had spoken to at the first address! I could hardly believe what I was seeing! She had had the brazen cheek to look me in the eye and profess she had never heard of Lorna Saporiti and here she was, bold as brass, walking out of her house. A young woman I presumed to be Lorna followed her, locking the door behind her.

As I walked towards the two women, Mrs Saporiti stared straight ahead, quite obviously avoiding eye contact.

As I reached them, I could not resist throwing at her, "Mrs Saporiti, I would not deny my child for anything or anyone in the world, let alone a measly television set."

Turning to Lorna, I told her I had just returned from reporting the theft of her television and video recorder to the police and they were now awaiting a telephone call from me to advise whether or not the equipment had been recovered. I went on to say she was virtually at the point of immediate arrest but, should she relinquish the television and video recorder there and then, no further action would be taken.

The trick worked. She immediately turned on her heel and took me indoors from where I collected both pieces without further problem.

However, unfortunately, not all the recoveries were so comparatively straightforward and there were times it was necessary to speak to a lot people along the line of the enquiry before the required result was achieved.

I found myself in Bath one day chasing a fraudster who had signed for nine video recorders using several names at five different addresses. Forged identity documents had been used and it was suspected he was probably selling the recorders on.

This individual and his activities had already been reported to the police but they seemed to be dragging their feet and, to date, no progress had been made.

As soon as the company passed me the paperwork, I immediately got cracking on it. Deploying myself in making enquiries at the installation addresses, I found two to be 'multi-occs' where none of tenants spoken to professed to know anything of our miscreant, another to be a derelict shop and yet another to be a terraced house occupied by three female students who informed me they had just moved in within the past few weeks.

My enquiries at the fifth and final address proved to be more productive. The lady answering the door informed me that the man I was seeking was a friend of her student son who had allowed him to stay there for a few days whilst she and her husband were on holiday. One of the holiday dates coincided with the installation date of a video recorder and I could see she was genuinely shocked when I informed her of this. She was adamant this had been done without her knowledge or permission.. She was still further shocked, as well as being very angry, when I informed her that the friend had used a false name. Her son had now returned to university, so was not available, but she was more than happy to give me the address of the man's parents.

On arrival at the given address, I found it to be a neat and tidy, semi-detached property on a decent class of residential area. I knocked on the door but there appeared to be no-one at home. On looking into the through-lounge window, I could see that the room was tastefully furnished but, obviously, there was no-one in. I decided to walk around to the rear of the house and knock on the back door. Still no reply. I looked through the picture window and now viewed the lounge furniture from a different aspect. Imagine my surprise when I saw a middle-aged man, crouched on all fours, hiding behind the couch! He was peeping around the corner of the sofa and looking towards the front window.

I tapped on the window and the man looked up, clearly startled. He got to his feet and, very sheepishly, opened the back door.

I started to explain to him the purpose of my visit but it wasn't long before it became very clear

98

I was at the wrong address. I was even in the wrong street! I had mixed up two very similarly named roads and had arrived at an address which had nothing to do with my enquiry. I made my apologies and left.

But why was the man hiding behind the couch? We will never know. I suppose he was just another debtor avoiding another creditor. How anyone would choose to exist in such an undignified manner, afraid to answer the door, beats me.

I was eventually able to confirm the rogue I was seeking still lived with his parents and, as the police already had the case in hand, I reported back my findings to them. I later heard they had raided the house with a search warrant and recovered all the equipment, together with several other recorders from another rental company. Apparently, our man was a budding entrepreneur making a nice few bob in the lucrative copied film market. He was subsequently given a suspended prison sentence for his illegal activities and, apart from a stop being put to his little caper, Alpha TV Rentals got its nine video recorders back which, as far I was concerned, was the main object of the exercise. As for being partially responsible for the man receiving the punishment, I rather looked upon that part of it as being an unfortunate by-product over which I had no control.

After about a month of recovering the company's tellies and video recorders in my part of the world, I was contacted by Alpha's head office and asked to join another investigator in

London for a week, a chap called Ron Douglas, who had been appointed to do a likewise job in an area south of the Thames. Due to the hostile nature of the populace in some of the districts, he was struggling to make an impression, so it was felt prudent to give him some back-up until he 'got on his feet', so to speak.

Depositing my trolley dolly at the Union Jack Club in Waterloo, my usual London stopover abode, I caught the Tube to Brixton, where I met up with Ron. I found him to be a dour, tough Yorkshireman with a cynical sense of humour and he started off by remarking he "wouldn't install a toothbrush let alone a television set" into the majority of the places he had visited so far.

We drove straight to a local authority housing complex, the notorious Stockwell Park estate, which can best be described as a holding cell for inmates awaiting their turn for a place in Brixton Prison. Walking along the third floor communal balcony, I realised from the sullen looks thrown our way by the multi-cultured mixture of residents we had made our first mistake; our smart dress identified us as the enemy. Definitely not the place to be seen in a suit, collar and tie, I thought.

Ron knocked on our target door and it was answered by an ethnic female of huge proportions. I stood slightly behind Ron, on his left shoulder.

"Yes? What is it you want, man?" she asked in a loud, authoritive voice.

"We are from Alpha TV Rentals. We've come to collect the TV and video recorder," Ron said.

100

"There's no television or video in here." she boomed.

"Yes, there are," Ron said, "They were installed 10 months ago and no payments have been made. Leon Eastman signed for them."

"I am Mrs Eastman. Leon is not in, but I'm telling you, man, he didn't sign for no television and video recorder," she said.

"I am sorry, but he did," Ron insisted, brandishing the contract.

With that, the woman turned and called over her shoulder, "Winston! Fetch de axe. I'm going to chop dis man's head off."

Luckily for Ron, Winston never materialised but the door was then promptly slammed in our faces and, needless to say, we didn't recover the equipment.

And neither did we make a single recovery the whole week, despite visiting several addresses every day. Some people just shrugged their shoulders nonchalantly and readily admitted they had sold the hired TV or recorder. Others denied all knowledge of the hirer, stating they had "just moved in" or "He's never lived here, mate". Such was the proliferation of serious crime on the types of housing estates we were visiting that a mere theft of a television or video recorder was trifling stuff.

This attitude was also symptomatic of the Metropolitan police approach to such matters and Ron, well knowing this, had apparently never attempted to report a theft of equipment. As he said, "What's the point? They won't do anything about it."

On the Thursday, feeling so frustrated with our lack of success, I tried to persuade Ron to make a report the police. If we had the evidence to back up our allegations, they would have to take an interest in at least one case, I reasoned. But he was dead against it. He said it was a waste of our time and effort. The police had bigger fish to fry.

At long last, I persuaded him to drive me to Waterloo police station where I intended to induce someone in the CID to take on board a job we had dealt with the previous day. Ron said he would take me there but only on condition that he would wait in the car outside. He said he would be too embarrassed to try and report something which he knew would be considered to be so inconsequential as to be positively risible.

The day before, we had knocked on the door of a young man who immediately 'put his hands up' and told us he had sold the equipment, a top of the range TV, to an unknown man he had met in a pub on the actual day it had been installed. Trying a little bluff, we had told him the matter would be reported to the police. His defiant reply was, "Please yourself. They know where I am."

Surely this would be something even a half-keen CID officer would be interested in? He only had to go along to the flat and Mr Smart Alec was his for the taking. A simple arrest and a feather in his cap. What could be easier?

Confidently, I walked up the steps and into the police station. Looking over his specs, the grey haired copper behind the counter gave me a withering look when I asked to speak to a CID officer. "What's it about?" he asked. "I can't bother the CID until I know what it is you want."

I outlined my story, at which he wearily picked up a pencil and said, "Tell me all about it. CID in the Met don't carry pens."

We never heard another thing.

This incident just about typified my week in London. It was a different world; a million miles away from my comfortable niche in South Wales.

Ron loved it. Though never a policeman, he had spent his entire investigating career in the capital and was well used to the immense diversity of its cultures and characteristics of its inhabitants.

He was welcome to it.

*

# Chapter Fourteen

## Mahmood Hussain Mattan

One day, in the spring of 1996, Bernard de Maid called me to his office to outline the intricacies of the new Criminal Appeal Act which had been enacted the previous year. The Act created a body called the Criminal Cases Review Commission, the purpose of which was to review instances where possible miscarriages of justice had occurred.

The Commission was now expected to become a vital element of the criminal justice system as it had been given the power to override the Appeal Court; the erstwhile last resort of anyone who thought he or she had been incorrectly convicted. More importantly, it was now possible to appeal against the conviction – and have it reversed – of someone believed to been wrongly executed by the State.

Of course, it goes without saying that the overturning of such a conviction is hardly of use to a man or woman who has been hanged but, at least, the reversal of the verdict does give a surviving relative the opportunity to claim recompense from the government in the form of an apology and financial compensation.

Mr de Maid went on to explain he was to be the very first lawyer in the whole of the UK to use the Act in respect of an executed person and that individual was going to be a man by the name of Mahmood Hussain Mattan who had been hanged in Cardiff Prison on the 3rd of September, 1952.

Mattan had been executed for the murder of a shopkeeper, 42 year old Lily Volpert, who had been found in her drapery shop with her throat cut. She had also been a moneylender and £100 was found to have been stolen.

A former seaman, Mattan was a 29 year old Somali national who was married to a white woman, Laura. He had settled in Cardiff and, at the time of the murder, was working at a local steel works. He and Laura were the parents of three young boys who had subsequently suffered gravely due to the ignominy of their late father being a convicted murderer and, last but not least, the rampant racial prejudice that existed at that time.

In the intervening years, Mattan had become somewhat of a *cause celebre* among the city's docklands community which was convinced he had been framed by a Jamaican called Harold Cover who had received £200 from the Volpert family as a reward for coming forward. This, despite the fact that Cover had earlier told the police the man he had seen outside the shop at the relevant time was another Somali, a Tahir Gass.

Mattan's trial at the Glamorgan Assizes at Swansea was a travesty, his own barrister calling him, "A half-child of nature, a semi-literate savage."

During our meeting, Mr de Maid gave me the task of scouring the Butetown area of the city in the search for any of the older residents who may have remembered the case and who could possibly give any useful information.

This I duly did, visiting the mosque, knocking on doors and taking statements from people who were around at the time and had personal knowledge of those involved in the case. In doing so, I collated plenty of hearsay evidence in Mattan's favour but nothing startlingly new which might be of use in positively proving his innocence. Most of the people I spoke to pointed the finger at either Gass or Cover as being the real murderer and it is worth mentioning at this stage that both these men were of the most disreputable character.

In 1954, two years after Mattan's execution, Tahir Gass was found guilty of the murder of a wages clerk. He was judged to be insane and was sent to Broadmoor and later deported to Somalia.

Harold Cover was a paid police informant who had a history of violence and, in 1969, was convicted of the attempted murder of his own daughter whose throat he tried to slash with a razor.

However, despite this lack of compelling evidence, Mr de Maid, in scrutinising the long forgotten case papers he had finally obtained from the South Wales Police, firmly believed there was sufficient anomalies in the original investigation and Mattan's subsequent trial to obtain a favourable result.

And so it proved. On the 24th of February, 1998, the case went before the Court of Appeal where the original trial was found to be "demonstrably flawed". The murder verdict was overturned and Laura and her sons were eventually awarded £725,000.

In receiving the monies, I wonder if Laura (who never remarried) and her sons felt truly compensated for the years of deprivation endured without a husband and father; the humiliation the sons felt when chased away by the Salvation Army officer as they tried to join in the singing with the other kids in the street or the abasement Laura felt when the bucket of water was thrown over her as she passed a neighbour's house.

If they did rejoice at their good fortune, the happiness they had found was certainly not long-lasting. The middle son, an alcoholic, was found washed up dead on a Scottish beach in 2003, the eldest son hung himself in woods on the edge of the city a few years later and Laura, herself, died of lung cancer in 2008.

So had justice finally been done and the correct verdict at long last been delivered?

I am not so sure.

In 2015, I had an experience which had the effect of reinforcing my already cynical mistrust of the criminal justice system.

I had just finished delivering a talk to a group of people from the U3A (University of the Third Age) and was gathering my files and equipment together when I was approached by an elderly lady who had been in the audience. The talk had been about another case history but, during the delivery, I had mentioned the Mattan affair, without going into much detail.

The lady's approach is a common occurrence at the end of talks, as members of the audience usually wish to ask questions or share their experiences on matters relating to the talk they have just heard.

But, the words of the conversation I had with the lady were so startling they are seared into my memory and I will repeat them exactly as they were spoken.

She said to me, "What makes you so sure that Mattan was innocent, then?"

I replied, "Well, for a start, the police produced as the murder weapon a broken shaving mirror which had no blood on it. It had not even been forensically examined. They also produced Mattan's shoes, which had minute traces of blood on them, but they failed to disclose to the court they had been bought second hand. Neither was the court told that Harold Cover, the main witness, was paid a reward by Lily Volpert's family for the evidence he gave."

I was now getting into my stride, "And, not only that, but a 12 year old girl, Lily Volpert's niece, saw a man standing outside the shop. This man was supposed to be Mattan, but the girl knew Mattan personally and she failed to pick him out on an identity parade."

What the woman said next made the hairs on the back of my neck stand on end.

"Well, let me tell you something," she said, "I *was* that 12 year old girl. In fact, I was 11 at the

109

time and I knew I would be sending a man to his
death and I couldn't do that. I had to go in the
room and touch him on the shoulder. I just
couldn't do it so I told the police the man I saw
wasn't in the line-up. But it was him alright"

This was, indeed, a breathtaking revelation.

So, was Mattan guilty or was he innocent?
Was he a helpless victim of officialdom's racial
prejudice, a tragic pawn chosen by indolent police
to tick a box? Or was he the real killer of Lily
Volpert, as intimated by her niece?

I will leave it to you, the reader, to decide.

*

# Chapter Fifteen

## The Lover's Letter

On many occasions, when attending an appointment to investigate an insurance claim, I would find not only the claimant awaiting my arrival but several members of the family, as well. I always considered this to be perfectly understandable, especially in the case of females, since I was aware of the anxiety and intimidation they might have experienced knowing they were about to be questioned closely by a professional person who, for all they knew, may well have been hostile to their claim.

This, despite when making the telephone appointment, I always introduced myself as a 'claims inspector' and always avoided the words 'investigator' and 'investigation', putting particular emphasis on the fact I was working on behalf of "*your*" insurers. Conscious that only a small proportion of claims merited a personal visit from an insurer's representative and that the claimant was probably also aware of this, I was forever at pains to try and allay any suspicions he or she may have had that the insurer had deemed there was something untoward with the claim and endeavoured to emphasise my impending visit was merely a matter of routine procedure.

The truth of the matter was that the vast majority of the claims I was sent to investigate could, at the outset, be seen to be ostensibly genuine. For instance, if the claimant was in his latter years, say older than 70, was a retired professional person who resided in a good class of area and there were no overtly suspicious surrounding circumstances, I would have thought the chances of him making a fraudulent claim to be extremely minimum. Thus, I was left with the suspicion that the insurance company handler had no more than randomly selected a sizeable bundle of incoming claims and sent them off, wholesale, to the agency with only the merest of glances into their contents. Thus, the onus lay on the investigator out in the field to discover what anomalies may have arisen in any particular file.

Notwithstanding the above, I was, of course, acutely aware that appearances could be deceptive so each claimant, regardless of age or status, nevertheless underwent the same rigid procedure at interview. As well, I was ever mindful it was imperative every assignment had to be approached with an open mind and dealt with on its own merits.

To illustrate this point, I can relate the instance when I once had occasion to interview 80 year old Lady Wills, of the W.D. & H.O. Wills cigarette empire (remember Woodbines and Players Navy Cut etc?), at her country estate near Bristol, in the presence of her husband, Lord Wills. I can honestly say I found them both to be genuinely polite and considerate and without a trace of false esteem or ego; a couple who treated me with every courtesy and respect, despite their stately stature.

There was little on the claim form submitted by Lady Wills to indicate the manner in which her Mini car had been stolen, apart from the bald statement, "Taken from public car park." Consequently, it was necessary to explain to her the purpose of my visit was to obtain the full facts of the theft in order her insurers could fully assess the claim and this she accepted without question or qualm.

We sat in the grand and tastefully furnished drawing room overlooking the vast, beautifully manicured gardens for over an hour, while I took down a full statement in writing, during which time we were served tea on a silver tray by a uniformed maidservant.

Lady Wills had driven her car to a town centre car park in Shepton Mallet at 8 o'clock one Monday morning where she was to rendezvous with her sister. They were intending to be collected by a coach to take them on a day's outing and her car was to be left in the car park. Before parking in a bay, she drove to a ticket machine and alighted to purchase a ticket. Intending to be away from the vehicle only momentarily, she left the keys in the ignition. Unfortunately, as she walked the few yards to the machine, a man jumped into the car behind her back and drove it away. The vehicle was later found, irreparably damaged, many miles away, but the culprit, having left his fingerprints all over the vehicle, was soon arrested.

The twist in the tail in this sorry saga is that the man, a serial car thief, had just been released from Shepton Mallet prison some 30 minutes earlier and was walking through the car park towards the bus station to catch a bus home when he saw - and seized - his golden opportunity!

Regrettably for Lady Wills, she had her claim rejected, her insurers ruling she had been negligent in leaving the keys in the ignition.

C'est la vie, I'm afraid.

But, back to the subject matter of the chapter title.

I travelled to Gloucester the following day to interview a lady in her late forties in relation to the theft of her car.

On perusal of her claim form along with the insurer's instructions, I found no hint of anything amiss. It was a straightforward overnight theft from outside the front of the house and the visit promised to be nothing more than routine.

On being shown inside to the drawing room, I found the whole of the family waiting for me; the claimant, her husband, her mother-in-law, and her two teenage children.

When asked to produce the vehicle's documentation, the lady brought out a large folder packed with servicing receipts etc, which was always a good sign. If the claimant was able to produce a full service history for the vehicle - as was the case in this event - it stood he or she in good stead with the insurer when it came to the valuation aspect as it was a positive indication the car had been generally well looked after.

114

As I took out my statement paper to record the lady's version of events, everything seemed to be proceeding smoothly

However, soon I was the one to feel intimidated! Every time I asked a question, it was invariably answered with another question from either the husband or mother-in-law, before the claimant had a chance to respond. "What do you want to know that for?" "What difference does it make what time she parked the car?" "What do you mean, 'did she lock the doors'?" etc. etc. And, of course, every question they fired at me had to be responded to with an explanation.

When I say I was intimidated, that is not exactly true. It was a more a case of being frustrated and flummoxed as, strictly speaking, the responses that were recorded on the statement – a legal document which she had to sign – were supposed to be the claimant's and hers alone.

However, the interview went along placidly enough without any of us showing annoyance and, after gathering up all the service papers and putting them in my briefcase, I left with the opinion the claim was probably genuine.

A couple of days later, I settled down at home to write my report to the insurance company and, in doing so, I spread out all the paperwork onto the table in front of me.

To my dismay, I saw, amongst the documents, the lady's driving licence, neatly folded into its transparent, plastic folder. It was the one thing I should not have collected. It should have been examined during the interview and the claimant's explanation for any anomalies that came to light recorded in her statement. Even now, I cannot fathom why I did not do this at the time. The only excuse I can offer is that I was probably a little confused in having to deal with the husband and mother-in-law and my concentration had momentarily lapsed. I was now irritated with myself that I had to disturb my report writing and take the trouble of going out to the post office to mail the licence by recorded delivery back to the claimant. Not only that, I had to type out a covering letter to go with it. This had to be done straightaway as, in the meantime, she would be unable to produce her licence to the police if she happened to be required to do so.

Never mind, I thought, it's no use crying over spilt milk. Just get on with it.

I took the licence from its sachet and started to open it out. As I did so, a folded sheet of notepaper fell out from within onto the table. As I opened it up, I saw it was a handwritten letter addressed to someone called 'Trevor'. It was signed by the claimant.

I settled back to read the letter and, although I was rather taken aback by its contents, I have to say I was also highly amused. Discretion dictates the words cannot be repeated *ad verbitum* but, basically, it could be seen the letter had been written in temper and scorn. Trevor was being told in no uncertain terms that their affair was now over. She was fed up with his lies and she now realised he had only wanted her for one thing etc etc. Coming out fighting with no holds barred,

116

she had liberally sprinkled the letter with the worst of swear words.

And, boy, what an imagination this woman had! What she was going to do to poor Trevor's genitalia if she ever set eyes on him again was nobody's business. It made my eyes water just to think of it!

I was now in a quandary. Obviously, I had to return this letter to its owner, but how? If I put it back in the driving licence and posted it off, how could I guarantee her husband would not open her mail? That would be truly disastrous for her and I would feel horribly responsible for the consequences.

I could destroy the letter and, without mentioning it, send the driving licence back on its own. But she might then notice it missing and wonder what I was going to do with it and perhaps worry I was up to something somewhat unscrupulous.

Finally, I decided my best course of action would be to telephone her and hope for the best that neither her husband nor any of her family answered the phone. If they did, I supposed I would just have to plead 'wrong number'.

However, as I recalled the woman had stated her occupation was a part-time assistant on her husband's fruit and veg stall at the local market and that she only worked a couple of days a week, I guessed I would probably be on safe ground if I called mid-morning.

Fortunately, the next day was a weekday, so surmising the children would be at school and hoping the mother-in-law would not answer the phone, I made my play. To be on the safe side, my scheme was to ask for the husband without identifying myself and, if he did happen to be at home, I would pretend I was a salesman calling from a call centre.

Luckily, the claimant herself answered the phone.

"Hello, could I speak to Mr Williams, please."

"I am afraid he is not at home at the moment and he won't be back from work until later this evening. Who is it?"

"Mrs Williams? Actually, it is you I need to speak to. It's the insurance chap who visited you the other day about the theft of your car. I picked up your driving licence by mistake and there was a letter in there addressed to someone called Trevor. I am going to send the licence back to you but what would you like me to do with the letter?"

"Oh, I forgot about that. The best thing to do is just rip it up."

Problem solved! I did just that. I sent the licence back, ripped up the letter and everyone was happy.

Her secret remained intact and Trevor never learned of the terrible fate that would befall him should he ever cross her path again!

*

# Chapter Sixteen

## A Fortunate Coincidence

**A** coincidence is said to be *"a remarkable concurrence of events or circumstances without apparent casual connection."*

Or, in simpler terms, a quirk of fate.

I think it is safe to say that each and every one of us without exception has, at some time in our lives, experienced an occurrence which we have thought to be so coincidental as to be hardly credible. How many of us have asked someone the time only for the voice on the radio or TV to announce the correct time before the other person could respond? How many times have we been in discourse with someone discussing a mutual acquaintance when the telephone has rung and it is none other than that very person who is calling? "Talk of the devil!" or, "How weird is that?" as a friend of mine would say.

Of course, there are degrees of coincidences, from the everyday trivia mentioned above to the life-changing event that happens but 'once in a blue moon'.

I am not quite sure which category the following anecdote would come into but, to me personally, it was a truly remarkable coincidence and certainly worthy of the telling.

I received a telephone call from a man introducing himself as an investigative journalist

119

attached to a national daily. He said I had been recommended by a TV company for which I had successfully carried out an investigation sometime in the past. He went on to explain he was currently involved in an enquiry on behalf of a Swansea based legal practise in which he may possibly require my expertise. Could we meet somewhere for coffee?

Never one to turn down the opportunity of an assignment, I, of course, readily agreed.

Meeting at the coffee shop in the Chapter Arts Centre, the "multi-artform space" which doubles as the Mecca of Cardiff's cultural anoraks, we sipped our drinks as Brian outlined his story.

A wealthy American lady had become enamoured with a chap from Gorseinon, a small town some 6 miles from the city of Swansea. Despite her only communications with him being via a dating site on the internet, she had sent him the rather tasty sum of $80,000. Fortunately, the payment had been forestalled by an astute local bank manager who, having suspected something untoward, had declined to accept the transfer until further enquiries had been carried out with the lady's bank. The US bank had then 'had words' with their client with the result that the transfer had been cancelled.

But the lady was still so smitten with the man and she could not let the matter rest. Through her attorney, she wanted to know anything and everything that could be discovered about the man's situation and background. Was he single and unattached, as he professed to be? Did he reside in a penthouse suite of a salubrious building overlooking a country park? Did he own a Jensen motor car? Was he a successful businessman who currently had a temporary cash flow problem?

Of course, I knew the answers to all these questions before I set out on my quest and, no doubt, these had been already spelt out to the lady by her bank manager and attorney. But the love-struck woman had to have her troubled doubts put to rest with solid proof.

I contacted the Swansea lawyers and, having agreed on a fee and reasonable expenses, I was given the go ahead.

Working with only the man's name and address and without the benefit of any official documentation, I surmised the enquiry was going to be a long, foot-slogging job, knocking on doors visiting pubs and local shops etc., therefore, I allocated a full day and evening to the assignment. Even then, as there was always the possibility it might be found necessary to return the following day to complete the task, I left that day free, too.

Making an early start, I took the M4 motorway and drove the 50 miles to the Gorseinon turn-off without stopping. Once off the motorway and thinking I deserved a little rest, I looked out for somewhere to have a spot of refreshment. Besides, not having a local road map, it would be a good opportunity to ask directions to the residential street I was looking for.

Passing a small retail park I noticed a Kwiksave store on the fringe and recalled that, sometime in the distant past, I had popped in there for something and noticed it had a cafe. This will do for me, I thought, as I pulled into the car park.

The cafe was virtually empty as I ordered a pot of tea and a light snack from the middle-aged, female behind the counter.

"Take a seat and I will bring it to you," she said. "It will only take a minute."

Settling down with my Telegraph, I decided that, as the lady was obviously a local person, she may be able to give directions to the address I was seeking.

As she arrived with my order and placed the plate on the table, I said, "You wouldn't know where Hermitage Road is in Gorseinon, would you?"

Astonishingly, she replied, "Yes, I do. I happen to live in that road."

"Well, blow me down!" I thought. How's that for a coincidence? Given that the last census showed Gorseinon's population to be 8,693, what where the chances of that happening?

But, it gets even better!

Trying to capitalise on my good luck, I said speculatively, "I'm visiting No. 37 to speak to a chap called Gareth Mullgrew, I wonder if I'll find him in."

The woman replied, "I live just up the road from them at No. 45. She's a Jehovah Witness and he left her and the three children and went off to Spain. She doesn't answer the door to anyone so it's no use you going there."

Seeing that the woman was a talkative person and there being so much I wanted to ask, I was anxious to carry on with the conversation but other customers had now arrived and were waiting at the counter.

Jumping in with both feet, I said, "I am making some enquiries on behalf of someone who is trying to contact Mr Mullgrew. Do you think I could pop around to your house later and have a chat?"

She replied, "Yes, that's alright. I finish at two o'clock. You could drop in after that, if you like."

I realise all this must sound rather implausible and you may well ask what woman would invite a strange man around to her house after such a short introduction but, on my word of honour, that is exactly what happened.

Spending the next couple of hours at my own leisure, during which time I covertly took some photographs of Mullgrew's house, I duly arrived at the address of my new found friend, bringing with me a bottle of white wine I had bought at a corner shop as a gesture of goodwill.

The woman welcomed me indoors and, pouring me a cup of tea, she soon began to chatter about Mullgrew.

"He's a right one," she said. "He used to have a garage selling cars in Swansea. He burnt it down and made a £20,000 insurance claim. He got two years in prison for that. Even his father who has a pub down the road is called "Billy Liar". He tells so many stories."

And so, on and on she went. Tale after tale. She gave me so much information that, even ignoring the tittle-tattle, I could have written a book.

But what the woman could not tell me was where exactly in Spain Mullgrew was and, although this piece of the jigsaw was not entirely essential, I thought if I had it, it would neatly wrap up the enquiry.

Once back at base, I turned to good old Duncan Facer once again.

"Duncan. I have a problem you may or may not be able to help me with. I am looking for a man living in Spain who has a bar somewhere over there. I haven't a clue in what area. All I can give you is his name and, roughly, the date he went there. Do you think you might be able to locate him?"

After one or two questions, he said, "Leave it with me, George, and I will see what I can do. I have a good contact there who may well be able to help."

A few days later and Duncan was back on the phone. "I have found your man, George. It is going to be costly, though. My chap in Spain had to scratch one or two backs," and, with that, he gave me the name and location of Mullgrew's bar.

I was now able to knock out a comprehensive report of my findings which, obviously, would have accordingly been passed on to the American lady; the lady who very nearly lost a small fortune.

I often wonder whether, after reading my report, she was still 'in love' with Mullgrew.

Which brings to mind that age-old saying, "There are none so blind as those who will not see."

*

# Chapter Seventeen

## Ruth Ellis

In the late spring of 1998, acting as his legal assistant, I accompanied Bernard de Maid to Swansea Crown Court where we successfully defended a famous Welsh rugby international on an assault charge. The charge had arisen as a result of a fracas in a night club following a big match when he had faced extreme provocation from rival supporters.

I say "we" because I was part of the team and I had previously spent a great deal of time and effort searching for, and collecting, evidence to support the player's defence. As a result of our - Bernard, the barrister and I – joint efforts, the player was justly found not guilty.

Earlier, sipping coffee in the court's cafeteria awaiting the jury's verdict, Bernard passed me a book on infamous murders and said, "I want you to read this book, George, and somewhere in there you should find the name of Ruth Ellis's next-of-kin. I would like you to trace whoever it is and make an appointment for me to visit and get some documents signed. Hers is the next miscarriage of justice we are going to tackle."

Ruth Ellis, of course, was the last woman to be executed in the UK. Her hanging caused outrage throughout the land, not just because she was a woman, but because of the gathering distaste among the public at large for the continuing aberration of the death penalty. Sadly, despite a concentrated press campaign and public demonstrations, she was hanged, nonetheless.

The murder for which Ruth Ellis was executed could be loosely described as a *crime passionnel*, although the deed was not committed in the heat of the moment but rather more cold-bloodedly calculated. Using a pistol given to her by Desmond Cussen, the man with whom she was living at the time, she shot her lover, David Blakely, after having travelled some miles to seek him out at his drinking haunt.

What was not revealed to the court at her trial was the fact that, having suffered a miscarriage some weeks before through being punched in the stomach by Blakely, Ruth was in a heightened emotional state. Fuelled by an excess of medication, her unstable mental condition was exacerbated by her heavy drinking in the hours preceding the shooting. Furthermore, she had been more than encouraged by a jealous Cussen who very obviously wanted Blakely off the scene.

As Cussen drove Ruth to the scene as well as supplying her with the gun, he should have also been charged for his complicity in the murder. This criminal omission was clearly due to either the incompetence of the police investigating officers or to their downright apathy.

This, then, was the basis on which the appeal was to be presented.

My initial research into the next-of-kin aspect revealed that Ruth had been born Ruth Neilson, the daughter of Arthur Neilson and Belisha Bertha, a Belgian lady, at Rhyl, North Wales.

She was the fourth of 6 children, of which there was now only one survivor, her 76 year old sister, Muriel Jakubait.

When Ruth was 17, she gave birth to a baby boy, who she named Claire Andrea ('Andy') McCallum, after his French Canadian soldier father but, having committed suicide from a drugs overdose in about 1978, he was, of course, immediately eliminated from our next-of-kin enquiry.

Ruth had later married - and subsequently divorced - a George Ellis, who had committed suicide by hanging himself in 1958, 3 years after her execution. There was a child from that marriage, Georgina, who, at the time of my research, was 47 years old.

Thus, it did appear that Georgina was Ruth's legal next-of-kin and, as she had somewhat of a high public profile, she would have been fairly easy to locate. But, my enquiries revealed her to have a rather chequered history and, after considering the unsavoury baggage she was carrying, it was eventually decided that she would not be a suitable person - for our purposes, at least - to be considered as next-of-kin.

Georgina Blackburn (her latest married name) had hardly known her mother. She was only 3 years old when Ruth was executed and, as her father had immediately had her adopted, she apparently now could not remember her. In the intervening years, she had made no effort to contact any of her blood relatives and so would be in no position to supply us with intimate background such as the family's side of the story in relation to the events leading to the murder.

Georgina had been married four times and was the mother of six children, either from her marriages or having been fathered by other men. She had convictions for drug abuse and was of a rather unstable character. She described herself as a 'model' and, despite her tenuous connection to her mother, had continuously hung on to her apron strings, touting herself around studios, for instance, and offering to play Ruth's persona, whenever she got wind of a film or TV documentary being produced. Needless to say, she never ever got the part.

What attribute she did have was rather a sweet singing voice and anyone caring to search Michael Barrymore on Youtube will find her being interviewed by him (interestingly introduced as "Georgie Ellis") on a clip in which she gives a decent rendering of "When I Fall in Love".

So, Georgina having also been eliminated, I looked towards Ruth's sister, Muriel Jakubait, and took steps to discover her whereabouts.

I have already mentioned earlier in this narrative my distant colleague, Duncan Facer, who was absolutely brilliant at tracing people and I decided to enlist his assistance in locating Muriel. At the same time, I asked him to also trace the whereabouts of Desmond Cussen as, without doubt, he would have some interesting things to say.

As usual, Duncan came up with the goods and, within a few days, I had Muriel's address in Woking and, with it, her ex-directory telephone number.

Unfortunately, Cussen had died in his late sixties in an ex-serviceman's rest home in Perth, Australia, taking his secrets with him. He had apparently fallen down a flight of stairs during a particularly severe attack of pneumonia and had broken his neck. As Ruth Ellis, too, died of a broken neck, some might consider that Cussen's terrible misfortunate was nothing short of poetic justice.

I rang Muriel as soon as I received her contact details and, on being informed of the nature of my call, she was absolutely delighted that, at last, someone was going to make a positive effort to exonerate her late sister. She had no hesitation whatsoever in inviting Bernard to meet her to complete the requisite documentation.

By the summer of the following year, the papers in our case were complete and the file ready to be presented to the Review Commission. A particular obstacle had arisen during scrutiny of the murder case file obtained from the Public Records Office at Kew inasmuch as we discovered a 50 years embargo had been put on some of the documents. This included the membership book of the Little Club, in Kensington, London, the last club Ruth Ellis worked in immediately prior to the murder. This meant that those particular documents could not be examined by anyone, neither press, legal profession nor public, until 2005.

Officially known as a 'D Notice', an embargo is more commonly used in cases such as spy trials etc. in which disclosure of evidence would represent a risk to national security. The embargo is normally a 30 year term, so why, in this instance, was it 50 years? And why would such a veto be placed on the Ruth Ellis papers at all? Anyone's guess is as good as mine but I believe I would not be far wrong in surmising that it was to protect the identities of certain prominent members of the 'Establishment' and, perhaps, even royalty, who were members of the club. This supposition may not be as far-fetched as it may seem, considering Ruth was a close friend of Stephen Ward, the celebrated physiotherapist to the high and mighty who, eight years later, figured prominently in the infamous Profumo affair.

In 2003, Ruth Ellis's posthumous appeal finally came before the Review Commission but, very disappointingly, and despite the efforts of the eminent barrister, Michael Mansfield, it was rejected.

An interesting postscript to this affair is that, in 2005, the 50 year embargo having now expired, Bernard de Maid, purely out of curiosity, contacted the Public Records Office to make arrangements to view the vetoed documents and guess what? He was informed the embargo had been extended for another 30 years!

Who are they protecting and why? We will never know in our lifetime.

Not in mine, anyway.

*

# Chapter Eighteen

## Travellers

During my career as a private investigator I had many dealings with the so-called 'travelling community' and I have to be forthright and say that, in my experience, I forever found them to be untruthful, and downright dishonest. I use the term 'so-called' in this instance because a lot of travellers have 'gone brick' and now reside in houses and many - probably the majority – live permanently on static caravan sites. However, despite the fact they no longer live a nomadic lifestyle they, nevertheless, still insist on being identified as 'travellers' and continue to embrace their age-old customs and cultures. The mere fact they are no longer itinerants has made not one iota of difference to their attitude towards the rest of society at large.

Actually, perhaps I am being a little disingenuous when I say all travellers are cunning and devious. They are not. Some just do not take the trouble to be crafty or scheming, being quite happy to be open in their contempt for the rules and regulations of the social order in which they exist. They are a law unto themselves.

As a police officer, long before I became an investigator, I had dealings with various travellers and, although I have already related this anecdote in my previous book, 'Coppers & Whoppers', I feel it is worth repeating here.

I had just recently joined the Coventry Police and had not long been let loose on the streets of that city without supervision. It was 6.30am on a dark winter's morning as I walked along a narrow, one-way street. A car approached from the opposite direction, travelling the wrong way. I stepped out into the road and, signalling the car to stop, I noticed there was no road tax being displayed on the windscreen. I pointed this out to the driver, a young man in his twenties, as well as referring to the one-way contravention. The conversation went as follows.

"This is a one-way street. You are travelling in the wrong direction."

"I am sorry, sir. I lost my way."

"You are not displaying a road tax disc. Do you have road tax for this vehicle?"

"No, sir."

"Have you got your driving licence with you?"

"No, sir. It is at home."

Taking a 'producer' from the top pocket of my jacket, I said, "You have seven days to produce your driving licence and insurance at a police station. What's your full name, please?"

"John Smith, sir?"

"What's your date of birth?"

"The 1st of January. I don't know what year."

"What's your address?"

"I'm a traveller. Our caravan is parked in a field near Leicester. I don't know the name of the road. We've only been there a week"

Knowing that I had no chance of ever hearing of or seeing 'Mr Smith' again, I resignedly buttoned the producer back into my pocket and said to the man, "On your way."

Fast forward to 1990 and I was given a theft claim to investigate in Swansea. The name on the file was a Miss Aideen Hoolaghan and the address given as The Presbytery, in Morriston, a residential suburb on the periphery of the city. The vehicle in question was a white coloured Ford Transit van which had been stolen mid-afternoon in the vicinity of a cafe during the time the claimant was inside having a meal. She was apparently unaccompanied at the time. Her age was given as 23 years.

The van had been purchased new, only a few weeks before the loss, for £14,000.

As I read through the claim form, lots of questions immediately sprang to mind. Why was the claimant's address a priest's residence which I knew to be an annex to the Catholic church in the tiny cul-de-sac road at the rear of the Morriston police station? What was a 23 year old woman doing insuring a Ford Transit van, bearing in mind the policyholder is supposed to be the main driver? Why was she driving the van alone at that time of day and why would she be having a meal in a cafe when, supposedly, she resided less than a half mile away?

Now, I have to very honest and admit that these questions only arose in my mind because I suspected the claimant was a member of the travelling fraternity. The name was a give-away, for a start, and I also knew travellers used

137

addresses like the presbytery as a postbox to collect their mail while travelling between sites.

The questions were raised in my mind not because of prejudice, but because the information submitted on an insurance claim form must be the truth and nothing but the truth, otherwise it can be adjudged to be fraudulent.

The reasons why the truth must be told would probably seem to be very obvious but the first question the insurer will raise in any suspect claim is "Why does the claimant find it necessary to tell an untruth? What is it we are not being told?"

We are not talking of downright fraudulent claims here in which property has not genuinely been lost or stolen, but rather of the information supplied by the claimant at the time of the policy's inception.

For instance what is the policyholder's age and occupation? Where is the vehicle normally parked overnight? It is not the first time I have visited someone who has purported to be 20 years older than his true age and it is not the first time a policyholder has stated his vehicle was parked in a garage overnight when, in truth, he didn't have a garage. It is important to understand the answers to these types of questions go a long way in determining the policy's premium and any discrepancy at the time of a claim will, at least, minimise the pay-out. At worst, they will cause the claim to be rejected.

I rang the mobile number on the claim form to arrange the usual appointment and it was answered by a female who confirmed she was the claimant. At her behest, we arranged to meet at the presbytery.

I arrived at the presbytery a few minutes before the appointed time and the door was answered by a middle-aged woman who introduced herself as the priest's housekeeper. She had never heard of Aideen Hoolaghan but, on explaining the purpose of my visit, I was invited to wait indoors in a small ante-room. The lady stated she was not surprised the address had been given as a rendezvous as travellers often used it "for all sorts of reasons".

A short while later, Ms Hoolaghan arrived, accompanied by a slightly older man. Once settled and the opening formalities over, I got down to the interview. Before doing so, however, I asked who the gentleman was and she replied it was her cousin, "Michael".

"The first thing I have to ask is, where do you live?" I said.

"I live here, sir," she replied.

"I don't think so. This is a presbytery," I countered.

"Yes, I do. I live here," she said.

"Where did you park the van every night before going to bed?" I asked.

"Outside the front of the house," she replied.

I then said, "Listen, I am a Roman Catholic. I know what a presbytery is. It's where the parish priest lives, and no-one lives with him, not even his housekeeper."

I then spelled out the importance of supplying a correct address to the insurers and went on, "Now, where do you really live?"

"On the old retail park at Llansamlet," she replied.

"Then why did you not say that in the first place," I asked.

"Because the postman won't deliver any mail there. We have our letters sent here," she replied.

And so the prevarications went on and on and the truth – whenever it did emerge – had to be patiently extracted bit by bit.

At the end of the interview, I drove to the address on the purchase receipt, a local Ford dealership, where the salesman confirmed its validity. He recalled the sale in detail. £14,000 had been paid in cash. During the conversation, we touched on the subject of 'cousin' Michael and he said, "That's not her cousin, it's her husband. I know them both well. He's bought a few vans from me in the past."

Why did she have to lie even about such trivia; something which would not have made one scrap of difference either way to her claim? The truth is, of course, travellers jealously guard there familial connections from the outside world. It is in their culture to disclose as little detail as possible of their personal affairs to those outside their community. Therefore, to them, prevaricating is a natural consequence of their upbringing.

Once back at my office at home, I set the wheels in motion to have an enquiry made with MID (Motor Insurance Data), the database shared by all insurance companies, and it turned out an Aideen Hoolaghan and her husband, Michael, as well as two passengers, had been paid £45,000, for injury damages in relation to an accident that had occurred in their home country two years previously.

I tried ringing the insurance company to obtain more specific details of the claim but was met with a stone wall. I was told the information was privy to that company, the claim files were stored at an unknown depot and frankly, they were not interested in the claim I was dealing with. I was told it was waste of their time to bother with something "in which they had no interest" and the £45,000 claim "must have been genuine otherwise we would not have paid out."

Consequently, I was never able to discover whether my Aideen and Michael Hoolaghan were the same people who had made the accident claim.

So much for all the hand-wringing and 'crack downs' we read about in the newspapers of insurance companies co-operating with each other in order to put a stop to fraudulent claims!

My report, outlining my misgivings and suspicions, was duly submitted but, without concrete evidence to prove any fraud, there was little doubt Aideen and her husband had another payday.

While on the subject of travellers, perhaps it may be of interest to illustrate a regular insurance scam perpetrated by 'the fraternity'; one which, in my time as an investigator, was extremely difficult to detect, mainly due to the poor liaison that then prevailed between the relevant licencing authorities. (With improved IT technology, the situation may well have improved since then but, somehow, I very much doubt it.)

A vehicle is purchased in the UK and registered with the DVLA and, at the same time, it is insured. After a reasonable period, during which time the premiums are paid on a monthly basis, the car or van is reported as being 'stolen' and a claim made to the insurer. The monies are paid out.

The vehicle, replete with its UK registration, is then taken to the traveller's home country where it is re-registered with that country's 'DVLA' and, of course, allocated a new registration number. Subsequently, it is then brought back to the UK where it is again registered with our DVLA at which time it is allocated yet another brand new registration document and number.

Voila!

How many times this exercise could be, and was, repeated with the same vehicle is anybody's guess.

A perfect illustration of our much vaunted 'linked-in partnerships' and 'joined-up government'.

*

# Chapter Nineteen

## John Howard Davies

From time to time, I regularly popped into a cafe in Crwys Road in Cardiff to treat myself to a slice of toast and pot of tea. I chose the cafe as it was situated on a main route from the city towards the outskirts and I used the break as an excuse to fortify myself ahead of a long journey to perhaps Bristol or Gloucester.

Invariably, as I struggled with the Telegraph crossword whilst sipping my tea, I would see an old gentleman sitting at his favourite table. Considering he seemed to be there every time I walked through the door, I guessed he probably used the cafe on a daily basis. On numerous occasions, I would see him scribbling in a small notebook and often wondered what it was he was writing.

One day, as I carried my tea from the counter, I impulsively asked if I could join him. He was the only customer in the cafe at the time, seated at the table next to the one at which I had intended to take a seat, and I thought I may as well sit with him for a bit of conversation.

The man, who introduced himself as "Ivor", was more than happy for the company and we were soon engaged in light conversation. I recall I was on my way to a mid afternoon appointment in Worcester that day and I had ample time to spare for a chat.

It wasn't long before Ivor and I were swopping notes and, on hearing of my profession, he immediately showed an intense interest. He said that he, too, was an investigator of sorts, although only in an amateur way, as his retirement hobby was researching the past lives of people who had died in unusual circumstances, particularly those who had perished in wars. Hence the notebook.

Ivor went on to tell me he had recently come across a grave in the nearby Cathays cemetery which had completely intrigued him and, try as he may, he just could not unravel the story behind the inscription on the headstone. His grandson had tried the internet in an effort to glean some information but had drawn a blank and although staff at the library near the cemetery had made a search through all likely literature on its shelves, it too, had come to nothing. Would I be interested in helping to put him out of his misery? So anxious was he to discover the answers, he promised he would be willing to pay me if I was able to come up with the relevant information.

Having already been given an outline of the gravestone's inscription, I was now myself sufficiently fascinated to assure Ivor I would help all I could. However, only on the proviso that whatever enquiries I could make would be in my own time and at my leisure. That way, no fee would be incurred and we could treat it as a joint venture. Of course, he readily agreed.

A few days later, Ivor and I met again; this time at the cemetery's gates in Allensbank Road, rather conveniently situated virtually opposite the entrance to the University Hospital of Wales. (Whether it was a deliberately strategic act to build the hospital across the road to the cemetery we will never know!)

Alighting from our cars, Albert led me the short distance to the plot in question and, although it was individually sited, as opposed to the war grave section, I immediately surmised it to be a war grave.

War grave headstones are distinctly simplistic in design and readily recognisable by their shape and limestone whiteness. Rectangular with an arched top, they are uniformly engraved with the crest of the deceased's regiment or, in the case of the Royal Air Force or Royal Navy, with the respective crest of the particular service.

The minimal inscription is, likewise, of uniform design, naming the service or regiment, details of the fallen one and the date and place of demise.

I have seen hundreds of war grave headstones in my time but never like the one pointed out to me by Ivor.

It was of remarkably similar design to that described above only, to my bewilderment, I saw that its inscription referred to a 12 year boy.

At the top of the stone, in place of the usual military crest, was the Boy Scouts emblem, the fleur-de-lis motif, with the word 'SCOUT' underneath and, below that, the name of the deceased, 'JOHN HOWARD DAVIES'.

From then on, the inscription read from top to bottom:-

ALBERT MEDAL
BRONZE CROSS
BY ACCIDENT 28TH MAY 1949
AGED 12 YEARS

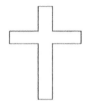

BELOVED SON OF
FREDERICK CHARLES
AND JANE DAVIES

Nothing more. Just the bare detail of the boy's identity and not a hint or suggestion of the manner of his passing other than, 'By Accident'.

This headstone raised so many questions it was no wonder Ivor was intrigued. Not surprisingly, my own interest was now intensified.

How did this boy die? What were the circumstances behind the awarding of the Albert Medal and Bronze Cross? How could a non-serviceman be buried in a war grave and how could someone be buried in such a grave when the death apparently occurred long after the end of the war?

Like Ivor's grandson, my first efforts to uncover this mystery was to resort to the internet

146

but, as he had already discovered, it proved fruitless.

'Google' had determined the term 'John Howard Davies' was almost exclusive to the famous actor and film producer of that name, the search producing countless websites devoted to him. (The reader will perhaps recall he played the part of Oliver Twist in the original film of that name.)

I next began to research the Albert Medal itself and to my initial delight, I found a book devoted to the medal's recipients. Alas, on further exploration, I found that it referred only to those heroically killed in the coal mining industry with no reference to any other holder of the award.

Luckily, what the site did have was the author's email address and so, in ever hopeful anticipation, I quickly pinged off a message to him, describing my dilemma. Most gratifyingly, he got back to me straightway with the full story.

John Howard Davies was a 12 year old schoolboy living in Sully, a suburb of Barry. He was an ardent Boy Scout and, on the day in question, together with a few fellow members of his local pack, he crossed the rocky causeway separating the tiny uninhabited Sully Island from the mainland.

On the way back, they were caught by the incoming tide and, although he made it ashore, three of his colleagues, all older than himself, found themselves cut off and in difficulty. Stripping to the waist, he courageously dived into the ever deepening waters and swam to their

147

rescue, as did a 14 year old bystander on the shore, a girl by the name of Margaret Vaughan. Together they were able to rescue the three boys. However, in doing so, John himself got into difficulties and was swept away by the strong currents. Sadly, he drowned and his body was not recovered until sometime later.

Both John and Margaret were subsequently awarded the Albert Medal; he posthumously and she being invested with hers by King George V1 at Buckingham Palace on the 1st of November, 1949.

John was also awarded the Scout Association's Bronze Cross and a particularly poignant rejoinder to this story is that it was his 13th birthday the following day. Thus, he perished on the brink of his approach to manhood, his whole life which lay before him being tragically torn from his grasp.

Incidentally, why John's headstone resembles that of a war grave, I was never able to find out. Neither have I been able to discover whether there are any rules governing the design of such headstones or whether it is merely a matter of choice of the next of kin. If so, I would presume John's parents may well have looked upon him as a brave young soldier who justly deserved to be remembered as a hero.

And who would care to disagree?

*

# Chapter Twenty

## More Case Histories

### *Trust Me: I'm a Doctor*

Occasionally, one comes across characters whose given circumstances, without even the minimum of investigation, immediately hit the eye as being hardly credible.

One such man was 45 years old John Grendon, of New Tredegar.

Mr Grendon had submitted a claim to his insurance company for the theft of his motor car, valued at £3000, stolen from outside the front of his house in Main Street.

I knew New Tredegar well, having visited there on numerous occasions in the recent past. I knew it to be a former mining village, a community which had seen better days prior to the demise of the coal industry. Without being disparaging to the good people of that town, I also knew it was highly unlikely a surgeon would be resident there, especially in School Street, a street of terraced housing, dating from the industrial pre-war days.

I say this because, browsing through Mr Grendon's claim form, I saw that he had declared his occupation as being that of a surgeon. I also saw that the space allocated for a contact telephone number had been left blank.

On calling BT Directory Enquiries, I was told there was no listing for a John Grendon in the whole of the Tredegar area. Not even an ex-directory listing.

Puzzled, I found this to be rather strange. Surely a surgeon would have a telephone at home? (These were the days before the advent of the mobile phone).

I rang Neville Hall Hospital, the main hospital serving that area, and was told they had never heard of a staff member called Grendon.

Not being otherwise able to make contact with him, I was left with no alternative but to write to Mr Grendon at his home address and inform him I would be there at a certain time on a given day the following week to carry out the requisite interview. Should the time or day be inconvenient, he was invited to either telephone or write me so that a new appointment could be made.

For me, this was a far from perfect situation. I certainly did not relish the thought, in the absence of a reply from Mr Grendon, of a 60 miles round trip to New Tredegar only, perhaps, to find no-one at home.

But I had no alternative and, as it turned out, indeed, he did not reply.

So, off I went and, during the journey up the valley, I had time to muse on what to expect. Suddenly, it dawned on me. Mr Grendon was probably a tree surgeon. Why did I not think of that before?

Arriving outside the front of the house and looking at the tatty net curtains hanging in the window, I was more than convinced I was right. What I was looking at was certainly not the residence of a surgeon.

The slightly built, weedy looking man who answered the door identified himself as Mr Grendon. He was decently dressed with collar and tie, although his cardigan was frayed at the elbows.

Sitting at the lace covered table in the old fashioned sitting room, we made light conversation about the actual theft before we got down to the serious business.

Without meaning any disrespect I was soon calling him by his first name.

Sometimes, it is like that in life. With some people you form an immediate rapport and others you call "Mr" or "Mrs" for ever more. It just depends on how your relationship, however brief, has developed.

"I am looking at your claim form, John, and I see you have your occupation down as a surgeon. What's that, a tree surgeon?"

"No. I'm a surgeon."

"A medical surgeon?"

"Yes."

"You perform operations on people?"

"Yes. I do."

"Which hospital do you work in?"

He didn't answer, but stared down at his feet.

Encouraging him to give me an answer, I went on, "If you are a surgeon, you must work somewhere. Where do carry out the operations?"

Now came the clincher which made it obvious John was more than just a little eccentric.

He blurted out, "I works *(sic)* in any hospital that wants me. I knows *(sic)* more about surgery that any doctor. I have all the books upstairs."

Now humouring him, I said, "Look, John, this claim form you have filled in is a legal document and whatever you put on it must be the truth. Your premiums are partly based on what you do for a living, so if you don't put down your true occupation, you are committing a fraud and the police could get involved. You understand that, don't you?"

I went on, "We don't want that, do we? Now let's be sensible. I know you are not a surgeon and you know you are not a surgeon. So what shall we put down as your occupation?"

A few seconds contemplation and John looked up and said resignedly, "Oh, just put me down as a doctor, then."

At that point, I gave up and decided it was futile to mention his occupation again. In any case, whatever he had been in his previous work life was immaterial as it was patently obvious he was now unemployed on a permanent basis. All the documentation was in order and, as there were no suspicions regarding the actual theft, I decided to finish off the interview and go home. It seemed clear John was a man who suffered from delusions and this was confirmed the following day when I spoke to a local policewoman who told me he was well known in the area and regarded as a local "character". She thought the theft was probably genuine.

On receipt of my somewhat sympathetic findings, no doubt John's insurers paid out in full.

*

## *Slip n' Trip in Maerdy*

Every few months, Ravenstones, the agency which supplied me with the bulk of my insurance work, would invite all its agents to its offices in Salford for a seminar. There were about twenty reps nationwide and it was a great opportunity to network and swap notes. Rod Bond, a former Greater Manchester Police inspector who ran the outfit, would give an excellent run-down on the latest information and edicts from the insurance world and, in this manner, we were kept up to date on current law and procedures etc. It was a thoroughly enjoyable and worthwhile day out, despite it being at our own expense.

One of the chaps I met there rang me one day and asked me if I was interested in taking on any work from a different source. Never being one to turn away potential income, I replied I was.

Denis explained to me that one of his clients, a company of solicitors based in Liverpool, had asked him if he knew of anyone in South Wales who would be interested in carrying out work for them in that area. The company had just been appointed to represent Rhondda Cynon Taff Council in order to investigate the sudden heavy

153

volume of 'slip and trip' compensation claims that had emanated in the recent past. Apparently, the council had been awarded an extra £1,000,000 by the government the previous year to bring its pavements up to scratch and, already, £500,000 had been expended on past injury claims.

On calling the contact solicitor at the company, he reiterated what Denis had said, stating the council were inundated with claims and he desperately needed an investigator to "sort the wheat from the chaff". As I had been recommended by Denis, who had worked for the company for many years, he was happy to appoint me without a formal interview.

The solicitor said he would start me off with a simple job. Would I go to the mining town of Maerdy and take photographs of a pavement on which a claimant had tripped in a crack, causing him to crash through the window of a house, gashing his arm? He said the council's insurers were satisfied the £3000 claim to be genuine so an investigation was not required and the photographs were merely needed to "tie up the loose ends." He added that the accident had happened two years previously and the insurers were now keen to "wrap it up."

I told the solicitor I knew Maerdy very well, particularly the road in question. It was a long street of terraced houses. What was the number of the house outside of which the fall took place?

"Ah, there you have me. There is no indication of that on the file and the underwriter originally dealing with the claim has since left the company.

You will just have to play it by ear and knock on a few doors to see if anyone can give you any information. I will post you the file today"

On my arrival mid-morning in James Street, in Maerdy, and faced with the dilemma of not even knowing which side of the road the incident had taken place, I anticipated the task was going to take some time. Consequently, I had allocated the whole of my working day to completing the job, so determined was I to make a good impression. This being my first assignment for the company, I obviously wished to encourage the solicitor's confidence in me.

Finding a convenient parking space half way along the road, I got from the car and knocked on the nearest door. I had to start somewhere and this seemed as good as place as any.

Call it luck or coincidence but, what happened next was truly amazing.

A young lady of about 18 answered the door.

"Good morning. I wonder if you can help me. I am from an insurance company and we are dealing with a claim from a young man who tripped on the pavement and fell through a window and injured his arm. I know this is the street but we are not sure which house it was. It happened a couple of years ago. You wouldn't know anything about it, would you?"

She replied, "Yes, I do know something about it. In fact, I know all about it. He didn't fall through the window, my father pushed him into it."

I was astounded, "Are we talking about the same thing? This man's name was Newbridge."

"That's right," she said. "Jimmy Newbridge. He was my sister's boyfriend and he had a fight with my father and my father pushed him through the window."

"Which house was it?"

"That one, painted yellow," she said, pointing to a house across the other side of the road.

"Were the police involved?"

"Yes. He got charged with assault and got sent to prison for 3 months."

I could hardly believe what I was hearing. Here was a man who has injured his arm in a fight, gets sent down for 3 months for assault and, when he comes out, he has the audacity to make a spurious claim against the council for supposedly tripping on the pavement.

You couldn't make it up!

I went to the yellow house and spoke to the occupant who confirmed everything the girl had told me. However, despite being invited indoors for a cup of tea and a chat, the man declined to make any sort of written statement.

I fully understood this. As I have observed earlier, these are close communities in which it is nothing short of an anathema to 'grass' on others.

However, what I did do then was to visit the local police station and there I was lucky enough to speak to a compliant uniformed officer who knew our Mr Jimmy Newbridge well. He copied all the papers in my file and promised me he would look into the matter.

This was good news as, usually, I got fobbed off by the police on the grounds insurance matters were nothing to do with them.

A few weeks later, I was informed that Mr Newbridge had been given another 3 months imprisonment for attempted fraud.

This was a fantastic result for me for, when the outcome got back to my new client in Liverpool, it earned me not only the kudos, but a steady stream of new cases with which to get to grips.

*

## The Supermarket Sandwich

Never again will I buy a sandwich from a supermarket.

I made an appointment with a young lady in Swansea to visit and take a statement from her regarding an accident she had witnessed.

Parking outside the terraced house at the appointed time, I noticed the front door of the property, facing onto the pavement, was partly glazed with frosted glass.

I rang the bell a couple of times and, receiving no reply at first, was about to return to my car to make a mobile call to the girl's number when I heard the faint sound of a toilet being flushed from inside the house. The blurred figure of a person could then be seen through the frosted glass coming down the stairs, directly ahead.

The door was opened and there stood before me was a chubby little woman in her late twenties. She was in the process of zipping up her jeans and fastening her belt.

"Come in," she said. "You must be the insurance man."

I was led into the front 'parlour' where a young boy of 8 years of age was lying sprawled on the floor, watching the TV. I could tell at a glance there was clearly something amiss with the poor child, either mentally or physically, by the way he was lying and his painfully slow movements.

Invited to sit at the dining table, I began extracting the accident file from my briefcase.

"Cup of tea?' the lady asked.

"That would be nice," I replied. "Thanks."

Getting down to business, the woman explained the circumstances of the accident which had occurred near to the town centre, an area I was not familiar with. During this time, before I had actually started writing, we also chatted informally and she began telling me of her personal circumstances.

She was a single mother and her son had been born with brain damage. Tragically, he was unable to walk without assistance and had difficulty in speaking and, of course, he needed constant care 24/7. Notwithstanding this, she was able to run her own catering business from home. She organised events, mostly children's parties, cooking up to 100 meals at a time. She did not drive but, her father, with whom she was in partnership, had a van and he made all the deliveries. Not only that, she had just been awarded a contract with a national supermarket chain, a household name, to supply sandwiches to one of its local stores on a daily basis.

Perhaps somewhat naively, I had always surmised supermarkets were supplied by large companies, operating from premises with pristine equipment and employing cooks and sandwich makers clad in lily-white overalls and hairnets with not a hair out of place, I could not imagine this lady supplying a supermarket from her tiny kitchen; a virtual cottage industry.

Despite being impressed with her enterprising and industrious attitude, I was a little sceptical.

"Where do you do the cooking and make the sandwiches?" I said, "You work from a premises somewhere, do you?"

"Oh, no," she replied, "I do it all in the kitchen. I have just had a new one fitted. Come and have a look."

She then led me proudly into the rear if the house and, I do have to say, despite it being just a normal sized, ordinary kitchen befitting of a terraced house, it did seem fit for purpose. The fittings being brand new, it was very neat and tidy.

Having eventually taken the statement, I explained to the woman my mandàte was also to visit the scene of the accident to take photographs and measurements of the road. Would it cause her any inconvenience to kindly accompany me there and show me exactly where the incident took place?

"Not at all," she replied and, indicating the boy, said, "I will just get him ready. He will have to come with us. I will just change his nappy," she said.

With that, she got onto her knees and, without a shade of embarrassment or concern for the lad's privacy, she proceeded to take of his trousers and change his diaper. She then got back to her feet and plonked the lot onto the table, right next to my half-drunk cup of tea. Goodness knows what was in the nappy but the whole incident was terribly unsavoury.

The diaper was left there, on the dining table, while she nonchalantly picked up the child and carried him to my car.

No doubt, the young woman was a very caring mother and she certainly lived and worked in challenging circumstances but, it goes without saying, her personal cleanliness and habits certainly left a lot to be desired.

From that day on, I have not been able to bring myself to buy a sandwich from a supermarket.

*

## Don't Tell the Wife!

Often, my mandate from insurance companies was to persuade the claimant to accept the underwriter's value of the stolen or accident-damaged vehicle. As it is a fact most people have an inflated value of their vehicles, this, naturally, had a tendency to be the cause of some contention.

On one occasion, I had reason to interview a small-time, self-employed builder in West Wales in relation to the theft of his car. From the outset, all the signs showed him to be a successful businessman. He lived in a beautifully converted barn, the restoration of which he had carried out himself in his spare time. Truly, it was a monument to his skill and good taste. However, as we sat in the easy chairs in front of the open, roaring fire, sipping the tea his wife had brought in from the kitchen, I noticed the fireplace to be nothing but a gigantic, gaping hole in the wall. Clearly, a work in progress. A part of the conversion that had yet to be completed, it was what could be described as 'a blot on the landscape'.

As I looked around admiringly, I casually asked Mr Morgan what he had planned for the fireplace.

"Shhh," he said, in a whisper, putting his fingers to his lips and looking over his shoulder towards the kitchen. "Don't let her hear a mention of the fireplace. It's been like that for two years, now. It will start her off again."

Changing the subject, I turned to the file. Mr Morgan was claiming for the theft an up-market car which he had purchased from a local dealer for £12000 cash as a birthday present for his wife.

It had been a snip, although I knew from my client's instructions that the car had been a write-

161

off prior to the purchase. Whether the builder was aware of this, I was yet to discover.

I asked him if he knew anything of the vehicle's history. Was he aware the car had been involved in a serious accident and that the previous insurers had sold it off as scrap? Under these circumstances his insurance company were asking him to accept an offer of £5000.

Mr. Morgan was genuinely shocked. He had been told nothing of this by the vendor and had bought the car in good faith. Apart from being stunned, he was angry with the dealer, whom he knew personally, that he had not been informed of this. Would I accompany him, there and then, to the showrooms, where we could both ask pertinent questions?

I welcomed this move as it was part of my assignment to glean as much information as possible in relation to the vehicle's background. Although the insurance company had learned through a simple HPI vehicle history check the car had been previously written off, they were keen to know the circumstances and the extent of the repairs subsequently carried out.

In those days, insurance companies did not co-operate with each other. If one company made an enquiry to another, client confidentiality or Data Protection would be quoted or that the relevant documentation had "been filed" in some unknown location or else it had been destroyed. In truth, they were just not concerned whether someone was committing a scam, as long as it wasn't against them. Now, the insurance companies, with their new-found access to MID, the aforementioned central database, fall over themselves to be seen to be supposedly co-operating in combating fraud and 'whiplash' injury. Of course, we all know this to be merely a concerted ruse they are using as an excuse to justify their continuous hiking of premiums.

But I digress.

Once at the forecourt from where Mr Morgan bought the car, he introduced me to the salesman who was equally shocked when informed it had been a previous write-off. He said he had sold it on behalf of a local vehicle repairer with whom he had regularly done business in the past without problem.

We made our way to the repairer who we found in his little workshop, a back street premises with barely enough room to swing a cat, and confronted him. He readily admitted having bought the car from the insurance company knowing it had been written off. That was what he did, he said. Bought damaged cars, repaired them and sold them on. He intimated it was up to the buyer to make suitable enquiries before he bought the car and accepted no responsibility whatsoever. In other words, *caveat emptor* more than adequately covered the situation.

Furthermore, he informed us of the circumstances under which the vehicle had been damaged, as related to him by the insurers. The previous owner had apparently been driving along a country lane behind a flatbed lorry carrying scaffolding when a pole had slid off the back and went straight through the windscreen, killing the driver.

"Oh, my God," groaned Mr Morgan, turning to me, "For Chrissake, don't tell the wife. She'll go bananas."

My mission now complete, I dropped him off outside the front of his barn, but not before he had tried to negotiate the underwriter's estimate.

"How can the car be worth so much less than what I paid for it? It was in absolute pristine condition. The repairs had been carried out with new parts. You would never tell it had been involved in an accident. It was beautiful. Otherwise, I would never have bought it for my wife."

I replied, "Put it this way. You see two identical cars on a forecourt. Both are the same make, colour and registration year and they have exactly the same mileage. Each is priced exactly as the other and you can't tell the two apart. They are like peas in a pod and you can't make your mind up which one to have. The salesman says, "It's difficult to choose, isn't it? But, this one on the right has been involved in a serious accident. Mind you, the repairs were carried out to such a high standard that, now, you would never know." "Which one would you choose?"

He replied, "The one on the left, of course."

"There you have your answer," I said.

*

164

# Chapter Twenty One

## The Saga of a Parker Pen

**W**ay back in 1958, as a young recruit in the Royal Air Force, I palled up with a Shropshire boy called Ron Barber. A young man who was to become my best mate for the next few years.

After training as wireless operators, we were eventually given our first overseas posting to Gibraltar where, for the following two years, Ron and I enjoyed many innocent adventures: visiting Spain on virtually a daily basis, as well as the odd trip across the Straits to Africa. The Rock itself was a paradise in those days, with bags of sunshine, sport and plenty of night life to keep the troops happy.

I remember our first trip to Tangier. Before the advent of mass tourism, a visit to such an exotic spot could only be dreamt of by the man in the street. Those were the days before the package tour, when Tangier was the exclusive haunt of playboy millionaires and film stars. Taking the "Mons Calpe" ferry to nearby Algerciras and then onwards to the 'dark continent' via the Spanish ferryboat, the "African Virgin", it was the most wondrous and exciting experience. It was no more than a weekend but those three days left us both with a lifetime of memories.

During this time, whenever I needed to write a special letter to the folks back home, I would invariably borrow Ron's dark-blue coloured

Parker fountain pen (the one with the golden arrow) and, as often as not, because we shared the same billet, it wasn't given straight back but left on my bedside shelf for days at a time.

I knew how much the pen meant to Ron. It had been presented to him on his enlistment into the RAF by his former colleagues in the Air Training Corps, in which he had reached the rank of sergeant, as well as gaining his glider pilot wings along the way.

In time, like all good things inevitably do, our tour of duty on the Rock came to an end and, unfortunately, on our return to the UK, Ron and I were posted to different parts of the country.

The postings were not simultaneous but weeks apart and, because of this, neither of us was aware of the other's new destination.

Weeks after settling into my new barracks, I was going through my tropical kit, preparing it for storage when, to my great surprise and utter dismay, I found the Parker pen tucked away in one of my jacket pockets.

However, despite being disappointed in myself in having failed to give Ron his pen back, it did not immediately seem overly important as I was confident we would meet up again in the near future.

But, as luck would have it, we didn't do so and, as time gradually rolled on, the chances of our crossing paths again gradually diminished and faded.

Over the next 40 years, although I moved house on numerous occasions, I always kept my

166

eye on the pen, certain that one day I would be able to return it to its rightful owner. In fact, it was boxed away with my cherished stamp collection, being used from time to time to neatly 'write up' and title each new set as the collection grew over the years.

Occasionally, I would have a go at tracing Ron, using the only facility available at the time, the telephone directory. Initially, hoping he had returned to his parent's home in his native Wellington following his demob from the RAF, I concentrated on that area. But, failing to discover a link with any of the 'Barbers' I did manage to contact, I was left with the conclusion he had obviously settled elsewhere.

Having already failed to elicit a forwarding address from the RAF Records office on the grounds of "confidentiality", I was left the daunting task of scouring the whole of the UK.

As time passed, I became ever discouraged but, despite this, the hope still lingered that one day it would happen.

Then, in 1998, the big breakthrough came.

I was now a Private Investigator and had acquired the magic disc I have mentioned earlier - the disc containing the whole of the UK Electoral Roll – and I now settled down to make a determined effort to find my old friend.

But, I soon found it was not quite so simple.

On surfing the disc, I discovered there were no less than 106 Ronald Barbers listed in the UK and, not only that, more than half of them had an ex-directory telephone number. I could see the process of elimination was going to be a monumental task!

However, noticing that many of the names were listed with a second initial, I wondered if Ron had a middle name. This would surely make my task easier. How could I find this out?

Well, I knew that the law allowed (and still does) any person to obtain another's birth certificate as long as the date and place of birth were known, and I did already knew these details.

I knew of them because I recalled Ron had once told me his birthday coincided with the name of a famous horse, April the 5th, which had won the Derby at Epsom in 1932. I also knew that he was a year older than me which, of course, gave me his birth year. I also knew that Ron had been born in Wellington and, subsequently, a simple telephone enquiry revealed that the Telford Registry Office held the Births, Deaths and Marriage Records for that particular town.

An application to that office, accompanied by the appropriate fee, and Ron Barber's birth certificate was duly delivered onto my doormat a few days later.

I opened the envelope and, hey presto!, the certificate told me my old mate's name wasn't just Ronald Barber but *Joseph* Ronald Barber! And this made all the difference for, on searching that name on my disc, only six persons surfaced with the name Joseph R. Barber – and four of them had available telephone numbers.

At the top of the list was a person of that name residing in Harlow in Essex. You can imagine the knot in my stomach as I dialled the number. A man's voice answered and, even after all the intervening years, I recognised it. It was him!

What a delightful conversation we had as we caught up on the respective paths our lives had taken since we had last said our goodbyes. (He later told me he had to sit down when he heard my voice.)

Not many weeks later, I drove up to Essex and Ron and I had a most wonderful reunion. He was now retired and his wife, Doreen, and their grown-up son and daughter had all taken the day off work to welcome me. We met at a local hostelry for lunch, after which we returned to their house to spend the rest of day reminiscing and mulling over old photographs.

But what of the Parker pen? Well, Ron was rather baffled when I produced it and admitted he could not recall where or when he had last seen it, even doubting, at first, whether it was his.

It took some time convincing him it really was his pen but, finally, something clicked in his memory. A sort of eureka moment. He shot upstairs and returned with a writing set presentation case in his hand and, on opening it up, there was the pen's matching propelling pencil!

Things certainly could not have turned out better.

Ron and Doreen subsequently visited Kay and I in little old Cardiff for a few days and we had the pleasure of showing them some of our tourist high spots. Not having previously been to Wales, they were terribly impressed.

Unfortunately, from then on, our contact gradually waned although we did exchange Christmas cards and we each made the odd telephone call. Despite this, Ron and Doreen did want to reciprocate our gesture and, over the next few years, Kay and I were repeatedly invited up to Harlow. But, unfortunately, every time suggestions were proposed for a suitable date for us to make the visit, it didn't seem to suit either us or them, so it never happened.

Then one day, out of the blue, I received a telephone call from Ron's son to say that, following a short illness, his Dad had sadly passed away.

So Father Time had finally caught up with my old pal and brought our era of friendship to a close.

But I am so gratified that, before it did so, I was able to give him the pleasure of being reunited with his long lost Parker pen.

\*

# Chapter Twenty Two

## Hysterical Women

**W**hat is it about some women that makes them so prone to hysterics?

Now, before the reader takes me to task for such an apparent crass and misogynous question, please allow me the time and space to qualify what I am attempting to say.

Not only that, but I hope the words I intend to write at the end of this chapter will leave no doubt as to what my true and sincere sentiments really are on this aspect.

Although the following narratives all have the female form at their centrepiece, I must hastily add that each and every protagonist could just have easily been a man.

Only it wasn't. It was a woman.

Many, many years ago, during my early days as a policeman, I attended an official lecture given by a psychiatrist in which he described a particular medical phenomena that he labelled "hysterical fits". He explained that it seemed only women were affected and the 'fit' was manifested by the person fainting for no apparent reason. This always occurred in the company of others and the diagnosis appeared to be that the victim sub-consciously craved attention. The recommended remedy was to state in a loud voice one's intention to depart the room and then leave the

171

affected person to her own devices. She would then apparently quickly regain conscientiousness and act as if nothing had happened.

Latterly, I have tried to research this so-called ailment and can find no mention of it in medical books or on the internet. This leads me to believe that if there is such a condition it has since been more precisely medically defined and is now probably treated in a more sympathetic and professional manner than hitherto.

Despite attending many issues of a 'domestic' nature and other related incidents involving women during my police career, I never once came across such a 'hysterical fit'. However, since embracing the profession of private investigating, I have to say I have, indeed, actually witnessed certain behaviour which, in less enlightened days, would have probably been described as hysterical fits.

One day, I stopped for a break in the services area on the old Severn Bridge at Chepstow and meandered into the retail shop to have a browse. There being few customers in there, the atmosphere was quiet, interposed only by the relaxing 'musak' emitting from the speaker system. Suddenly, a loud crashing noise from behind me grabbed my attention and, on spinning round, I saw that a middle-aged lady had tumbled backwards into the confectionary display, sending chocolate boxes flying into the air. She was now lying on her back, seemingly unconscious.

The counter assistant immediately rushed over and attended to the woman, at the same time instructing another girl to summon a first-aider.

The first thing that struck me about the woman was that, despite it being a chilly day, she was not wearing a coat, cardigan or jumper. Her summery dress was short sleeved and she wasn't wearing tights. Stranger still, she was empty-handed, with no sign of handbag or purse.

There were a few other men in the shop apart from myself – probably three or four – all smartly dressed in suits and collars and ties, who appeared to be, typically, reps or businessmen.

The first-aider, a responsible looking lady, arrived and took charge of the situation, waving smelling salts under the woman's nose at the same time calling out, "Is anyone with this lady?"

The other men just looked on, no-one offering a response. The first-aider called out again but still no reply was forthcoming from the onlookers.

Then, in a loud, firm and authoritive voice she called out, "Now, come on. She's with *somebody*. She has no coat or handbag and no money. Which one of you is she with?"

With that, one of the men stepped forward and rather sheepishly volunteered, "Er, she's with me. I picked her up a few miles back."

As he said this, the fainted lady started to show signs of coming round and, at that point, I left, chuckling to myself as I walked to my car.

We will never know what the good Samaritan's intentions were when he picked up the woman but, one thing is for sure, he had certainly lumbered himself with something he hadn't quite bargained for!

On another occasion, I was working with Bernard de Maid, acting on behalf of a convicted murderer whose appeal we were preparing. He was a homeless 'wino' who had been with a group of fellow alcoholics enjoying a few bottles of cider on a summer's evening on the flat roof of a low-rise block of flats when an argument had broken out. One of the group had been stabbed, resulting in his death, and our client had been deemed responsible.

Bernard and I had visited the man in Cardiff Prison and, despite his drunken state at the time of the incident, he had vehemently denied being to blame.

"I wants (*sic*) a truth machine," he had shouted out as the warder led him away at the end of our visit.

My remit was to go to the block of flats and make door-to-door enquiries in an effort to find impartial witnesses.

It was late summertime and, deciding an evening visit would give me the optimum chance of finding people at home as well as giving them time to finish their evening meal, I arrived at the flats at about 8pm, just as dusk was falling.

The lights had not yet come on in the block's downstairs corridor and, as I walked into the main entrance, I momentarily had to adjust my eyes to the gloomy dimness.

I knocked on the first door I came to and it was opened by a young lady of about 18 years. The

174

lights were out in the room behind her and she stood in virtual darkness. I introduced myself and said, "Good evening. I wonder if you can help me. I am making enquiries about a serious assault that took place about two years ago on the roof of these flats when a man was killed. You wouldn't know what happened, would you?"

Without a breath of a word in reply, the girl suddenly dropped to the floor in a faint and, lying in a motionless heap at my feet, she appeared out for the count. Not seeming to be injured in any way, she just lay there, still and silent.

Immediately recognizing what I thought to be a 'hysterical fit', I quickly decided that discretion was the better part of valour and, leaving the girl where she had fallen, I beat a hasty retreat back to my car and drove straight back the way I had came.

Please don't misunderstand me. I am the first to help a damsel in distress. But not on my own in a dimly lit corridor with not another soul in sight to witness what is going on. There was no way I was going to hang around and lay myself wide open to the possibility of some sort of spurious accusation.

I subsequently left that part of the enquiry for another day, this time returning in broad daylight and giving the young lady's flat a wide berth in doing so.

Hysterical fits aside, I have to say I have been on the receiving end of a frenzied scream on more than one occasion in my time and the perpetrator has always been a woman. However, again, I accept it could have just as easily have been a man.

I recall visiting a retired engineer living in a very desirable, up-market bungalow on the outskirts of Swansea. He had had his car stolen and I had been mandated by his insurers to make the usual inquiry.

Inviting me indoors, he led me straight into the tastefully furnished drawing room and immediately made us both a cup of tea. Settling into the deep armchair, I made myself comfortable whilst we made jokey chit-chat.

Then we got down to business and, after examining his documents, I started to take his statement. Where and at what time did he last park the car? Did he lock the doors and set the alarm? etc. He appeared happy and relaxed and responded without query or hesitation.

Suddenly, his wife appeared in the doorway, screaming at the top of her voice. "Why don't you get off your backside and get out and find the person who stole my husband's car instead of asking him all these stupid questions?"

I was flabbergasted and speechless. What had I said or done to deserve this outburst?

The man got up and led his wife back into the kitchen, placating her at the same time, "Calm down, dear. Calm down, please. The man is only doing his job."

As he returned to the armchair, his eyebrows went up, his eyes rolled and we carried on where we had left off without any further interruption.

On another occasion, I went to investigate the theft of a large van which had been taken overnight from outside the front of a modest terraced house.

The claimant, a young man of about 30 years, answered the door and introduced me to his wife, who settled herself down to sit in on the interview. During the preliminary conversation, he explained the brand new van had only recently been purchased and fitted out with storage racks. He was a plumber and, following redundancy at a local factory, he had invested his £12,000 redundancy pay-off in the acquisition of the van and top-of the range tools. Now, some low-life thief had robbed him of his livelihood. He was, understandably, devastated and desperate for his claim to be processed quickly so that he could buy replacements and get his life back on track.

As we got into his statement, I happened to pose a rather innocuous question but, in doing so, I inadvertently referred to the van as a car.

At this, the wife suddenly leapt up and screamed out, "It's a van, not a car! You just don't care, do you? It's our living. It's nothing to you, is it? To us, it's our life and to you it's just another claim." Bursting into tears, she ran from the room.

The man rushed out after her and returned a short while later. When he did so, I apologised profusely. I understood the stress they must have been under, what with children and a mortgage to pay. A young, hard-working couple trying to make their way in life. It was none the wonder my slip of the tongue had upset her. I promised the man I would do all I could to see that his claim was progressed as soon as possible. Immediately on return to my office, I called the claims handler at the insurance company and, on learning of the exceptional circumstances, he assured me that as soon as he had sight of my report, the claim would receive his immediate attention. Hence, I knocked out my report that evening and ensured it was in the post box the first thing the following morning.

As I asserted at the beginning, some women are prone to hysterics. But that is surely because they are simply *different* to men. It does not make them any better or any worse. Just different. Therefore, they react differently to different situations. Sometimes women are more reasoned than men and, certainly, there is ample evidence the male is more aggressive and belligerent in his general behaviour. Otherwise, we probably wouldn't have so many wars.

However, as I cannot claim to be a psychologist, I am not qualified to comment further on this aspect of humanity. Suffice it to say I can do no better than quote the celebrated philosopher and author of 'Lord of the Flies', Sir William Golding:

"I think women are foolish to pretend they are
equal to men; they are far superior and always
have been. Whatever you give a woman, she
will make it greater. If you give her sperm, she
will give you a baby. If you give her a house,
she will give you a home. If you give her

178

food, she will give you a meal. If you give her a smile, she will give you her heart. She multiplies and enlarges whatever is given to her. She is the greatest gift that God ever bestowed on Man."

And I couldn't agree more!

*

# Chapter Twenty Three

## Eddie Browning

One day in 1998, I received instructions from an insurance company to contact and interview one of its clients in relation to a traffic accident. The circumstances of the incident were apparently that the insured person, a farmer, had reversed his horse-box into a car parked in a field at a country market, causing damage, and had left the scene without stopping. A witness had taken the registration number of the horse-box, called the police and a prosecution was now pending. The client's stance was a complete rebuttal of any involvement in the accident and, in fact, a denial that the horse-box had been outside the confines of his farm at any time on the day in question.

The name on the paperwork showed the client to be an Edward Browning and his address given as a farm near to the town of Lampeter in Ceredigion, some 90 miles from my base.

The name meant nothing to me whatsoever and, on my initial telephone call to Mr Browning, I was given no hint he was anything other than the normal claimant requiring to be interviewed. However, he did come over as a somewhat overly affable person who gave the distinct impression he was more than keen to give his side of the story. The conversation was friendly, to say the least. So friendly that, at its termination, Mr Browning said, "By the way, call me Eddie. And

181

we had better meet in the car park of the rugby club in Lampeter. My farm is very remote. I would have a job to find it myself - and I'm ex-SAS."

Those last few words came over as rather a little pretentious and I have to say it did make me slightly sceptical. As an ex-serviceman, I know that SAS men just do not brag about having being in the regiment. On the contrary, it is their unwritten law never to unnecessarily disclose they have been so and, in my experience, I have found that those who do boast about being in the SAS invariably turn out to be nothing more than braggarts and charlatans. Moreover, on replacing the receiver, I also thought, "Eddie Browning. That's the same name as the M50 murderer. That's a coincidence."

Eddie Browning had been convicted and sentenced to life imprisonment in 1988 for the rape and heinous murder of the pregnant 22 year old Marie Wilks, whose car had broken down on the M50 motorway, near Worcester.

As Browning lived not too far from Cardiff at the time, the case received lots of local TV coverage but, 10 years having elapsed in the meantime, it was now in the distant past. In any case, as I was under the impression that he was still in prison, I never imagined in a million years he and our client could be one and the same person.

As I waited in the car park of the rugby club at Lampeter, a Landrover drove in and I have to admit I *was* struck by the general resemblance of the man who stepped from it and approached my car to the TV images I dimly recalled of Eddie Browning. But it was no more than a fleeting thought and, from then on, it did not cross my mind again.

I followed the Landrover to the 'farm', which turned out to be little more than a smallholding: a semi-dilapidated farmhouse and stables on a couple of acres of rough land, nestling in a secluded nook along long, narrow and twisty lanes. Mr Browning had been right; I would never have found it on my own.

Following introductions to his young wife and their newly born baby, we settled down in front of a roaring fire to begin the interview.

The crux of the matter centred on whether the horse-box in question had been involved in the non-stop accident, regardless of who had been driving and 'Eddie' insisted it had not. He was the vehicle's sole user and he was adamant neither he nor the horse-box had left the farm that day. I pointed out to Mr Browning that an independent witness had seen the incident and had noted the registration number of the horse-box. This had been checked out by the police with the DVLA and they seemed to be satisfied it was his vehicle. His reply was that it was all a pack of lies and a vendetta was being waged against him.

"For what reason would anyone wage a vendetta against you?" I asked.

"Because they don't like me up here," he replied.

183

"Why should they not like you?" I further asked.

Looking at me with an incredulous expression on his face, he blurted out, "Because I'm Eddie Browning! I'm the man who did 8 years for the M50 murder. I got off on appeal but they still think I did it around here."

What a revelation! So he was *the* Eddie Browning after all! To say I was astounded is an understatement. Once I had recovered sufficiently to take it all in, Mr Browning had no hesitation in regaling me with the story of his arrest, his time in prison and the subsequent appeal which led to him being exonerated of the crime. Not only that, he insisted on bringing out a video tape recording of an hour long TV documentary featuring himself, the theme of which was the continuous police harassment he was suffering. According to him, whenever a murder occurred anywhere in the country he was the first person they came and arrested.

Did Eddie Browning commit the M50 murder? The law says he did not but, as he was acquitted on appeal on a technicality regarding (rather bizarrely) a hypnotised witness, there is room left for doubt. As Eddie died in May, 2018, taking his secrets to his grave, perhaps we may never know.

Perhaps advancements in DNA may one day unearth fresh evidence bringing us an irrefutable final conclusion as to the true identity of the man who raped and slit the throat of Marie Wilkes.

Who knows?

\*

# Epilogue

The life and times of a private eye, as I have known them, have gone forever. Together with traditional policing, they have vanished into the dim mists of time. The 'bobby' on the beat with his whistle, Raymond Chandler's 'gumshoe', the rubber heeled door-knocker and the shady guy in the grubby old raincoat have all been confined to history's dustbin.

They have been replaced by a bewildering array of technology; the computer with its apps, Facebook, Twitter and Instagram etc. and the now readily available, sophisticated, surveillance gadgetry makes obsolete the need of the physical presence of the investigator. Miniature covert cameras, listening and recording devices transmitting in real time, GPS tracking and a multitude of databases have all contributed to the demise of the now defunct foot-slogging enquirer.

Time marches on with ever improving ingenuity. So it has been since time immemorial and so it ever will be. I fully accept this – I have had my day and enjoyed it but now it is time for a new breed of investigator to take over the reins where the dinosaur has left off.

As I say my good-byes to the profession and its newcomers, I wish them well and trust they will enjoy the same good fortune as I have experienced myself.

\*

Printed in Great Britain
by Amazon

18518816R00109